AMATEUR WINEMAKER RECIPES

Edited by C. J. J. Berry

FIFTH IMPRESSION

August 1970

Cover designed by G. Hodgson
Cartoons by Rex Royle
Some recipes by Cyril Shave

Printed by Standard Press (Andover) Ltd.
South Street, Andover, Hants   Tel. 2413

SBN 900841 10 9

About this book

THIS book makes no pretence to be a detailed instruction manual, for that function is better performed by two other books in this 'AW' series—"First Steps in Winemaking" (6/-), a book for the beginner, "Progressive Winemaking" (15/-), and "Scientific Winemaking" (12/-), manuals of more advanced winemaking.

All it sets out to do is to record in a convenient form some of the more striking, successful and unusual recipes that have appeared in the "Amateur Winemaker" magazine in the course of two or three years, and which many readers have asked should be published in book form. Since they are intended to be a representative selection we have also included some of the more popular and commonly-made wines, so that the book covers a wide range of recipes.

With their help you will be able to turn out a selection of wines as appetising as they are different; and we hope you enjoy making them as much as you enjoy drinking them. It is hard to say which is the more delightful process!

C. J. J. BERRY

Modern Winemaking

THE fact that there are today well over 300 Winemaking Circles in the British Isles alone, to say nothing of those in Canada, Rhodesia and "down under," each with a flourishing membership, is an indication of the extent of the modern revival of interest in our ancient craft, for most of these have been formed in the last decade.

Helping to promote and encourage this present day interest is "The Amateur Winemaker," a monthly magazine with a circulation currently of over 18,500, selling throughout Great Britain, and distributed to enthusiasts in the U.S.A., Africa, and other countries as far afield as Japan and the Yukon. Many specialised books on the subject have been written by recognised authorities and other factors in the popularisation of winemaking have been the friendliness and infectious enthusiasm of home winemakers, and the willingness of education authorities to include the subject in their syllabus for evening classes.

Winemaking probably originated by accident when early man or woman first discovered the pleasant flavours and intoxicating effects of alcoholic fruit juices fermented by natural yeasts from over-ripe fruit stored in primitive containers.

Wine was certainly an everyday commodity to the ancient Egyptians, Greeks, Cretans, Romans and other Mediterranean peoples several thousand years before Christ. The Bible contains many references to vineyards, grapes, wine presses, bottles and wine—Noah is said to have been the "first" winemaker, and his story is a salutary one!—and wine became one of the essentials of good living, hospitality and merriment, as evidenced by the Biblical story of Christ's miraculous provision of the wine deemed essential at a wedding feast.

Today, although all famous commercial wines (each with its own characteristic flavour) are essentially made from numerous varieties of grape grown in many different parts of the world, more and more amateur winemakers are learning to experiment and improve wines made at home from almost every type of fruit, grain, vegetable, leaf, flower and herb, until these products now compare favourably with, and are sometimes vastly superior to, many commercial wines.

It is true to say that, thanks to the continual study, research and experimentation of recent years by many winemakers, including those with a scientific background and thorough knowledge of chemistry, yeasts and the processes of fermentation, winemaking knowledge has made big strides. Unlike other fields, in winemaking the experts' findings have been made available to the public in numerous books containing an introduction to winemaking and countless well proved recipes of interest to both the beginner and the expert. "First Steps in Winemaking" published by the "Amateur Winemaker," is a typical example.

With only the simplest basic equipment anyone can produce wine of excellent quality, flavour and alcoholic content to suit palates of all tastes, from light dry dinner wines to rich sweet dessert and social wines.

Most of the utensils can be found in any kitchen—a large saucepan or kettle for boiling (stainless steel, aluminium, or sound enamel ware, but not iron, brass or copper), a large crock or bowl (white, not lead, glaze) bottles and corks, and a wooden spoon.

Other items which will be found useful are glass 1-gallon bottles or jars, fermentation traps to keep the wine from contamination, a yard of rubber tubing for siphoning, a corking machine, a large plastic funnel for filtering (the larger the better) and, if you wish to go further into the "mysteries," a hydrometer to help calculate the strength of your wines.

Notice that your utensils, apart from the boiler and crock already mentioned, should be of glass, non-resinous wood (oak ash or beech), plastic or white glaze pottery (lead glaze can lead to poisonous results).

Everything must be kept scrupulously clean by the use of boiling water or baking in the oven, where possible, or by the use of a sterilising solution which can be used to rinse out bottles and apparatus. This is easily made by dissolving six Campden tablets and $\frac{1}{4}$ oz. citric acid in a pint of water. (Campden tablets are merely fruit preserving tablets).

Any wine consists of:
1. Flavouring,
2. Water,
3. Sugar,
4. Yeast, and
5. (hardest to obtain!) Time.

All that happens when yeast, a living "plant," is put into a sugary solution, is that it feeds upon the sugar, converting it roughly half to alcohol and half to carbon dioxide, by weight, so that one finishes up with a pleasantly-flavoured alcoholic drink.

We extract the flavour from fruits and vegetables by boiling them, by soaking them in cold water, or by a combination of the two (*i.e.* pouring boiling water on them and leaving them to soak).

As regards sugar, one need only remember that $2\frac{1}{4}$ lb. per gallon is required to produce a wine with sufficient alcohol to keep, 3 lb. will usually produce a strong dry wine, and more, up to 4 lb., will produce a wine correspondingly sweeter, since the excess sugar will not be converted to alcohol.

There are many types of yeast. Some winemakers stick to baker's or brewer's yeast, but we would recommend either a good-quality wine yeast or a good granulated yeast. All will make wine, of varying quality, and usually the decision as to which type to use resolves itself into a matter or personal preference.

In all the recipes in this book use $\frac{3}{4}$ oz. baker's or brewer's yeast per 1 gallon of liquor, or 1 level teaspoonful of a good granulated yeast. With wine yeasts full instructions are supplied.

Beware of "No yeast" recipes. No liquor will work *without* yeast; it means that you are relying upon the natural yeast in the fruit, or, if you have killed that by the use of boiling water or sulphite, on any "wild" yeast which happens to be in the air . . . and the gamble may not come off.

Yeast nutrient can be used to "boost" the action of the yeast and is particularly recommended in flower, mead and other wines where the liquor is likely to be deficient in certain trace minerals One can obtain nutrient ready made up but most chemists will prepare it to this formula:

Tartaric acid, 80 grains; ammonium sulphate, 60 grains; magnesium sulphate, 8 grains; citric acid, 55 grains; potassium phosphate, 30 grains. This is for 1 gallon of mead or two gallons of wine.

If you cannot obtain this, use per gallon a teaspoon of ammonium phosphate (ask for di-ammonium hydrogen phosphate) obtainable from most chemists.

Wine, it should be noted, must have some acid, and also some tannin, for astringency, if it is to be correctly balanced.

The fermentation should be in two stages, the first vigorous one when the yeast is multiplying itself to the required level, and needs air for the process, and the secondary, quieter one, when it is converting sugar to alcohol, during which time air should be excluded; it is then that one should employ the modern device of a fermentation lock.

This will act as a barrier to the vinegar fly, and to the vinegar bacteria which are the winemaker's biggest enemies.

If they infect the wine it will turn to a peculiarly flavoured vinegar, fit only for the drain. In the early stages, therefore, the wine must also be kept closely covered.

Knowing all this, we can summarise the winemaking process thus:

1. Extract flavour from ingredients by boiling or soaking in bowl or crock.

2. Add sugar and yeast and ferment from 10 to 20 days in a closely-covered bowl in a warm place (65-75°).

3. Strain off, put into fermentation bottle, and fit fermentation trap, filling to within an inch of bottom of cork. Temperature: about 60°. This fermentation will be much softer and will proceed for some weeks, but eventually all bubbling will cease.

4. "Rack," *i.e.* siphon, the cleared wine off the "lees," or yeast deposit at the bottom of the jar. This should be repeated about a month later, and usually a third racking after a further three weeks is beneficial. By now the temperature should have been reduced to 60° and the wine should be quite stable, with no risk of explosions!

5. Bottle when wine is about six months old and corked securely. Bottles are then stored, on their sides, preferably in a room of about 50° temperature.

Do . . .

Keep things very clean.

Keep air away except during first few days, and even then keep brew closely covered.

Use fermentation trap for secondary fermentation.

Keep fermenting bottles full to within 1 in. of bottom of cork.

Strain wine well initially or it will be hard to clarify.

Keep a book and jot down all you do, so that you can repeat it.

Use new corks.

Don't . . .

Allow vinegar flies to get at brew.

Ferment in a metal vessel.

Put wine in old, damp bottles, or it may be infected.

Let sediment lie at bottom of bottle or it will impart a bad taste to the wine.

Rush a wine: give it time!

Forget to stir the "must" twice daily.

Use finings or filter unnecessarily; most wines will clear of their own accord, given time.

Throughout the ages wine has been offered as a gesture of hospitality to one's friends and guests and somehow this aura of goodwill seems to embrace all winemakers too. Some prefer to work on their own, others appreciate the advantages to be gained by membership of a Wine Circle, where problems and recipes can be discussed, products sampled and comment invited, and speakers lecture on such diverse subjects as the history of glass bottle making or the effect of the sun upon the sugar content of fruit.

Wine Circles can also offer their members many social events and outings, and the advantages of bulk buying, saving heavy postal costs on individual parcels. If you wish to know the address of your nearest Circle write to: "The Amateur Winemaker," North Croye, The Avenue, Andover, Hants. There is also a National Association of Amateur Winemakers, which organises an annual conference, a feature of which is a wine show which may have as many as 3,000 bottles exhibited.

Winemaking is certainly the "in" hobby of the late 1960's. Some winemakers are content to make a few gallons annually, others drink at least a gallon a week and give a lot away to friends as well, they might make 100 gallons a year.

A bottle of home-made Apple Wine was even used by Mrs. Healey to launch the nuclear-powered submarine "Renown"!

You, like thousands of others, will find winemaking a stimulating, enjoyable, and rewarding pastime, and the recipes in this book will suggest to you some wines which are excitingly different.

Your health, dear reader!

RECIPES

Agrimony and Banana

Ingredients:

    1 lb. fresh agrimony herb (or 1 small packet dried herb) (agrimony eupatoria)
    4 oz. dried bananas (or 2 lb. fresh bananas including skins)
    1 lb. raisins (sultanas, prunes, dates, etc., will do)
    3 lb. sugar
    ½ oz. citric acid (or 3 lemons no pith, in lieu)
    1 cup strong cold tea (or a pinch of grape tannin)
    Water to finally make up 1 gallon of must
    Yeast nutrient and activated wine yeast

Method:

    Place the chopped herb and fruits together with the sugar into the initial fermentation vessel. Pour in the *boiling* water and stir well with a wooden spoon to dissolve the sugar. When cool add the citric acid, strong tea, and yeast nutrient. Introduce the activated wine yeast, and ferment on the "pulp" for 10 days, stirring the must twice daily with a wooden spoon and keep it closely covered. Then strain, for secondary fermentation, into a fermentation vessel and fit air lock. Leave to ferment in the normal way, racking as necessary in due course.

Agrimony and Rice

Ingredients:

    1 small packet dried agrimony herb (acrimonia eupatoria) (1 lb. fresh herbs or 2 ozs. dried herbs)
    1 lb. wholemeal rice (or wheat, barley, etc.)
    ¼ lb. raisins (or sultanas, currants and figs, etc.)
    3 lbs. sugar (or 4 lbs. honey)
    ½ oz. citric acid (or 2 lemons, no pith, instead)
    1 tablespoon strong tea (or 1-10th oz. grape tannin)
    Water to make up 1 gallon of "must"
    Yeast nutrient and activated wine yeast

Method:

Place the herb, grains, chopped dried fruit and sugar into the initial fermentation vessel. Pour in the *boiling* water and stir with a wooden spoon to dissolve the sugar, etc. When cool add the citric acid, strong tea and yeast nutrient. Introduce the activated wine yeast and ferment on the "pulp" for 10 days, stirring the "must" with a wooden spoon twice daily ensuring that the "must" is closely covered. Then strain, for secondary fermentation, into fermentation vessel, and fit air lock. Leave to ferment in the normal way, racking as necessary in due course.

Other interesting rice wines are detailed in "130 New Wine-making Recipes."

American Fruit Wine

American winemakers in California commonly make wines heavier in body than is customary in this country, where fruit is perhaps not quite so readily available in large quantities. They also commonly pasteurise. Here is a recipe—by Rockridge Laboratories, of Oakland, California—that readers might like to try:

FROM BERRIES

With berries like Strawberry, Raspberry, Loganberry, Blackberry, Boysenberry, etc., use in these proportions:
10 lbs. fruit, 3 pints water

With currants, gooseberries and elderberries:
10 lbs. fruit, 6 pints water

Method:

Add fruit into enamel or stainless steel container, add the water, heat slowly, with occasional stirring, just to boil. Turn off heat, let fruit cool to room temperature (preferably overnight). Then drain through cheesecloth, collect juice in enamel or stainless steel container, or glass bottle. Press remaining "pulp" only lightly. Combine all juice in glass or wood container to prepare for fermenting into wine. Proceed about it as follows:

To each 1 gallon of juice, add

1½ lbs. sugar, mix to dissolve
1 crushed Campden tablet
1 yeat nutrient tablet
1 yeast starter (3-4 ozs. per each gallon juice)

Ferment under sterile gauze or cotton cover, or use fermenting trap, at room temperature (70–80°F.). In 1–2 weeks, or whenever fermentation has ceased, let settle a few more days. Then rack clear wine into freshly cleaned bottles, full. Again let set upright, loosely corked, preferably in refrigerator at 35–50°F. When settled clear, rack off clear wine, sweeten to taste, heat in enamel

or stainless steel container to 140°F, bottle hot, cap or cork tightly. Set aside to cool and age. If no sweetening in last step is desired, wine may be stored in full containers without pasteurising.

When quantity of fruit is too large to first make the juice as directed, the fruit is lightly mashed, water added as recommended. Then to each gallon of mashed fruit/water mixture, add sugar, yeast nutrient, yeast starter, etc., as for the juice above, and add **double** the amount of sodium bisulphite, or 2 tablets (1 gm.) per each gallon. Let ferment under gauze cover. When fermentation looks vigorous (1–2 days), drain all juice from "pulp," press only lightly. Combine all drained and pressed fermenting liquor and continue fermenting under it gauze or cotton plug, or fermenting bung, same as for fermenting the juice. Follow from here the directions as outlined for handling the wine from juice.

Apple Wine

Ingredients:

    12 lbs. mixed apples
    2½ lbs. sugar
    1 gallon water
    Yeast

Method:

Make this wine in quantity, it is so easy. Measure out 12 lbs. of apples, wash them quickly in running water in a colander, and then chop, mince, or pulp them. We use a crusher, but you can do the job with a piece of timber or half a brick in a tub, or use a mincer, but this last is rather hard work. Drop the pulped apple into a polythene dustbin and when you have done 12 lbs. add 1 gallon of water. Then do another 12 lbs. and add another gallon, and so on until your receptacle is full. Then add one level teaspoon of granulated yeast for each 12 lbs., and stir well in. Cover closely and leave for seven days, stirring vigorously each day and pushing down the cap of pulp which forms to keep it wet. At the end of the week beg, borrow or steal a fruit press. Place a 1 gallon jar (as a measure) below the spout of the press and into the neck of it place a large funnel, holding a nylon sieve. Use a small saucepan as a "baler" and start filling the basket of the press with pulp and juice. The juice will run through freely, be strained, and gradually fill the 1 gallon jar. As each jar is full, plug it with cotton wool and stand it to one side, replacing it with another. Naturally, when the press is full of pulp, one starts pressing, and continues until the pulp is almost dry; then that pulp is thrown away and the basket gradually refilled.

Now count your 1 gallon jars, and for each jar
sugar into your dustbin, carboy, or other fermenting v
in all the juice in the one-gallon jars and stir well to c
sugar. Fit fermentation lock and ferment, rack and b
usual way. The wine is usually ready for drinking afte
months but is infinitely better if left in wood for a further year.
And before someone points out to us that this recipe breaks all the
rules we'll say "We know—but it always works!"

Apple and Rasin

Ingredients:

> 6 lbs. mixed apples (or more), eating, cooking and crab apples if
>   possible
> 1 lb. raisins (or sultanas, apricots, etc.)
> 2 ozs. dried bananas (or 2 ozs. dried rose hips/shells)
> 2½ lbs. sugar (or 3½ lbs. honey)
> ¼ oz. tartaric acid ("B.P." quality)
> ¼ oz. citric acid (or 3 lemons, no pith, in lieu)
> ¼ oz. ammonium sulphate ("B.P." quality)
> ¼ oz. pectozyme
> Water to finally make up 1 gallon of "must"
> Activated wine yeast

Method:

Grate up the apples (including skins and cores, and place
these with the dried fruits and sugar into the initial fermentation
vessel. Pour in the *boiling* water and stir well with a wooden spoon
to dissolve the sugar. When cool add the tartaric and citric acid,
ammonium sulphate, pectozyme and strong tea. Introduce the
activated wine yeast and ferment on the "pulp" for 10 days,
stirring the "must" twice daily with a wooden spoon, and ensure
the "must" is closely covered. Then strain, for secondary fermentation, into fermentation vessel, and fit air lock. Leave to ferment
in the normal way, racking as necessary in due course.

Apricot (dried)

Ingredients:

1 lb. dried apricots	Pinch of tannin
½ oz. pektolaze	Yeast and nutrient
2½ lb. sugar	Flat teaspoon citric acid

Method:

Wash apricots well in hot water. Soak overnight in ½ gallon
water. Next day bring to the boil and boil for five minutes. Lift
apricots out carefully, strain into colander. Put all liquid in polythene bucket, cover well and put right away from kitchen. When

13

cool, and pectolase, stir in sugar, put into gallon jar, fill to shoulder with cold water, add tannin, acid, yeast and nutrient, insert air lock and proceed as usual.

Apricot and Fig

Ingredients:

1 lb. dried apricots
1 lb. dried figs
1 lb. sultanas (or raisins, currants, etc.)
2 ozs. dried bananas
¼ oz. citric acid (or 3 lemons, no pith, in lieu)
½ pint strong tea (or a pinch of grape tannin)
2½ lbs. sugar (or 3 lbs. honey)
Water to finally make up 1 gallon of "must"
Yeast nutrient and activated wine yeast

Method:

Chop up the dried fruits and place these together with the sugar into the initial fermentation vessel. Pour in the *boiling* water and stir with a wooden spoon to dissolve the sugar, etc. When cool, add the strong tea, citric acid and yeast nutrient. Introduce the activated wine yeast and ferment on the "pulp" for 10 days, stirring the "must" with a wooden spoon twice daily, ensuring that the "must" is closely covered. Then strain, for secondary fermentation, into fermentation vessel and fit air lock. Leave to ferment in the normal way, racking as necessary in due course.

Artichoke (dry wine)

Ingredients:

4 lbs. artichokes (tubers)
1 orange
1 lemon
1 gallon water
2½ lbs. white sugar
½ lb. raisins
Yeast and nutrient
1 cup cold strong tea

Method:

Slice the artichokes and add the thin peel of the citrus fruit and the chopped raisins. Place all in the water and boil for 30 minutes. Strain the liquid over the sugar, stir well to dissolve and add the juice of the orange and lemon and a large cup of strong tea. Allow to cool, then add the yeast and nutrient. Leave two days, closely covered, in a warm place, then put in fermenting jar and fit sherry trap. Leave to ferment out, rack and bottle as usual. A sherry yeast seems to improve this wine.

14

Balm and Almond

Ingredients:

> 1–2 ozs. packet of dried balm herb (or 1 lb. fresh herb)
> 1½ ozs. bitter almonds
> 2 ozs. dried banana (or 3 lemons, no pith)
> 1 lb. raisins
> 3 lbs. sugar
> ½ oz. citric acid (or 3 lemons. no pith)
> ½ pint strong tea (or $\frac{1}{16}$ oz. grape tannin)
> Water to make up finally one gallon of must
> Yeast nutrient and activated wine yeast

Method:

Mince the almonds and simmer in the water for 30 minutes: place the chopped bananas (and skins if fresh bananas are used), raisins, sugar and balm herb into the initial fermentation vessel. Pour on to these the hot almond liquor and almonds, stir well with a wooden spoon to dissolve the sugar, etc.

When cooled down to 70°F., add the citric acid, strong tea, and yeast nutrient. Introduce the activated wine yeast and ferment on the pulp for 10 days, stirring each day with a wooden spoon, and ensuring the must is closely covered.

Then strain into the secondary fermentation vessel and leave to ferment under the protection of a fermentation lock, racking as necessary in due course.

Balm and Greengage

Ingredients:

> 1 quart balm leaves, including stalks
> 2 lbs. greengages (stones removed)
> 1 lb. wheat, barley or maize
> 1 lb. raisins or sultanas
> 3 lbs. sugar
> 2 lemons or oranges (½ oz. citric acid may be used in lieu)
> ½ pint cold tea
> 1 gallon water
> Activated yeast and nutrient

Method:

Pour 1½ pints of water over the grain and leave to soak overnight. Next day run the grain (being careful not to lose any liquid) and raisins through a coarse mincer, and put into crock with the balm leaves, chopped greengages and the juice of the lemons or oranges. Pour over them the gallon of water, *boiling*. Cover closely and leave for three days, stirring daily. Then strain, add the cold tea, sugar, yeast and nutrient and stir thoroughly to dissolve the sugar. Pour into fermenting jar and fit air lock. Ferment in the usual way and rack when clear. An excellent dessert wine with full body and attractive aroma.

Banana

Ingredients:

3 lbs. bananas	2 gallons water
1 lb. raisins	2 ozs. yeast
8 lbs. sugar	

Method:

Peel the bananas before weighing them. Cut them up, together with the raisins. Then boil them in the water for about 15 minutes. Strain carefully, add the sugar, and allow to cool. When the temperature has reached 80°F (26°C.) add the yeast and allow to ferment 14 days before bottling. Leave the wine six months.

For a different flavour, dates may be used instead of the raisins.

Barley

Ingredients:

1 lb. barley	1 orange and 1 lemon
1 lb. raisins	Yeast
3 lbs. Demerara sugar	1 gallon hot water
1 lb. potatoes	

Method:

Put barley through mincer and then put it into a crock with the chopped raisins, scrubbed and chopped potatoes, fruit juice, fruit rinds (no white pith) and sugar. Pour over the hot (not necessarily boiling) water and when cool add yeast. Leave to ferment (closely covered) in a warm place for three weeks, stirring daily. Then strain into fermenting jar and fit trap. Leave until wine clears and fermentation ceases, then siphon off into clean bottles and cork. This is a smooth dessert wine of about 14% alcohol by volume.

Barley and Apricot

Ingredients:

    1 lb. barley (wheat or maize)
    2 lbs. dried apricots (or 6 lbs. fresh apricots, stoned)
    1 lb. raisins (sultanas)
    3 lbs. sugar (4 lbs. invert sugar)
    ¼ oz. citric acid (or 2 lemons, no pith, in lieu)
    ½ pint strong tea (or a pinch of grape tannin)
    Water to finally make up 1 gallon of must
    Yeast nutrient and activated wine yeast

Method:

Prepare the grains by soaking overnight and then by mincing them together with the dried fruits. Then place these together with the sugar into the initial fermentation vessel and pour in the *boiling* water, stirring well to dissolve the sugar. When cool (70°F) add the citric acid, strong tea and yeast nutrient, and introduce the activated wine yeast. Ferment on the "pulp" for 10 days, keeping it closely covered, and stir with a wooden spoon each day. Then strain into secondary fermentation vessel, fit air-lock and leave to ferment in the normal way, racking later as necessary. If fresh apricots are used they need merely stoning and cutting up—they should not be minced.

Barley and Grapefruit

Ingredients:

    1 lb. barley (wheat or maize)
    3 or 4 grapefruits
    1¼ lbs. raisins (sultanas or figs)
    ½ oz. dried elderflowers (do not exceed this amount)
    3 lbs. sugar (or 4 lbs. invert sugar)
    ½ oz. citric acid (or 3 lemons, no pith, in lieu)
    ¼ pint strong tea
    Water to finally make up 1 gallon must
    Yeast nutrient and activated wine yeast

Method:

Grind the barley and dried fruit in a mincer, having soaked the grains in a pint of water overnight. Infuse the dried elderflowers, as in tea making, using two pints of water, and bring to boiling point. Place the minced grains, dried fruit and sugar into the initial fermentation vessel, add the elderflower liquor, and the remainder of the water, which should be almost boiling. Stir well with a wooden spoon to dissolve the sugar, etc. When cool (70°F) add the grapefruit juice and finely grated skin from one grapefruit (no pith), citric acid, strong tea and yeast nutrient. Introduce the activated wine yeast. Ferment, closely covered, for 10 days, stirring each day with a wooden spoon, then siphon, using nylon strainer into secondary fermentation jar. Fit air lock and leave to ferment in the normal way, racking as necessary. This recipe permits much licence in variation of quantities of ingredients providing the dried elderflowers are not used in excess of quarter pint.

Barley and Limeflower

Ingredients:

> 1 lb. barley
> 2 ozs. dried limeflower
> 1½ lbs. figs (dates, sultanas or currants)
> 2 ozs. dried rose-hips/shells
> 3 lbs. sugar (or 4 lbs. invert sugar)
> ½ oz. citric acid (or juice of 2 lemons)
> $\frac{1}{10}$ oz. grape tannin (or 1 cup strong tea)
> Sufficient water to make up finally 1 gallon of must
> Yeast nutrient and activated wine yeast

Method:

Wash the grains, then soak them overnight in 1 pint of the water. The next day mince the grains in a domestic mincer, using the coarsest holes and then place the grains into the initial fermentation vessel together with the chopped fruits, bruised flowerheads and sugar. Pour on to these the *boiling* water and stir well with a wooden spoon to dissolve the sugar, etc. When cool (70°F.) add the citric acid, tannin, and yeast nutrient. Introduce the activated wine yeast and ferment on the pulp for 10 days, stirring each day with a wooden spoon, and ensuring that the must is closely covered. Then strain into the secondary fermentation vessel and leave to ferment under the protection of a fermentation lock, racking as necessary in due course.

Barley and Orange

Ingredients:

> 1 lb. barley (wheat or maize)
> 12 oranges (mixed sweet, Seville, etc.)
> 1½ lbs. raisins (or mixed dried fruits)
> (½ pint of grape concentrate may be used instead of raisins)
> 2½ lbs. sugar (or 3 lbs. honey)
> ¼ oz. citric acid (or 2 lemons, no pith, in lieu)
> ¼ pint strong tea (a small pinch of grape tannin)
> Sufficient water to finally produce 1 gallon must
> Yeast nutrient and activated wine yeast

Method:

Grind the barley together with the dried fruit (if used), having soaked the grains in a pint of water overnight. Place the minced grains, etc., together with the sugar, into the initial fermentation vessel and pour in hot water. Stir well with a wooden spoon to dissolve the sugar, etc. When cool (70°F.) add the orange juice (and grape concentrate if used) and finely grated skin (no pith) from one orange, also add the citric acid, strong tea and yeast nutrient. Introduce the activated wine yeast. Ferment, closely covered, for 10 days, stirring each day with a wooden spoon, then strain into secondary fermentation jar. Fit air lock and leave to ferment in the normal way, racking later as necessary. If a full orange tasting wine is desired, add *after* the first racking one bottle of "curacao" (red or white) or "orange" extract from the T. Noirot range of extracts.

Beetroot

Ingredients:

6 lbs. beetroot	1 lemon
1 gallon water	3½ lbs. sugar
Yeast	

Method:

Wash the beet, and cut them into slices, cooking gently in the water until tender, but not mushy. Strain on to the sugar and stir well to dissolve, then add the juice of 1 lemon. When cooled to blood heat add yeast and leave, closely covered, in a warm place for 24 hours. Then put into fermenting bottle, fit an air-lock and leave to ferment out. Bottle when clear and stable.

Red Fodder Beet

Ingredients:

4 lbs. beetroot
1 gallon water
Yeast and nutrient
3 lbs. sugar
¼ lb. raisins
2 teaspoons lemon juice

Method:

Scrub the beetroot thoroughly. Cut off any green that may be left on them. Cut into thin slices and boil in the gallon of water until just tender. Strain off into jar containing the sugar and raisins. Stir for a few seconds until the sugar is dissolved. When cool (70°F.) add the yeast nutrient, and lemon juice. Stir well. Leave for seven days, closely covered. Strain off into fermenting jar and fit air lock. The beetroot can be placed in jar containing half vinegar and half water, with salt to taste. (Makes excellent table beetroot).

Beetroot and Carrot

Ingredients:

2¼ lbs. beetroot
2¼ lbs. carrots
1 lb. figs (or raisins, sultanas, dates, etc.)
2 ozs. dried bananas (or 1 lb. fresh bananas including skins)
3 lbs. sugar (or 4 lb. invert sugar)
1 level teaspoon citric acid (or juice of 3 lemons)
½ pint of strong rea (or ½ teaspoonful grape tannin)
Water to make up 1 gallon of must
Yeast nutrient and activated wine yeast

Method:

Scrub the carrots and chop them up and simmer until tender in 3½ pints of water. Scrub the beetroots and remove any green stalks, slice thinly and simmer in 3¼ pints of water. Place the chopped fruits and sugar into the initial fermentation vessel and strain into this the hot beetroot and carrot liquors (the carrots may be eaten) and stir well to dissolve the sugar, etc. When cool (70°F.) add the citric acid, strong tea and yeast nutrient. Introduce the activated wine yeast and ferment on the "pulp" for 10 days, stirring each day with a wooden spoon, ensuring that the must is closely covered. Then strain into the secondary fermentation vessel and leave to ferment under the protection of a fermentation lock, racking as necessary in due course.

Beetroot and Clove

Ingredients:

3 lbs. beetroot
3 or 4 cloves
1 lb. figs (or raisins)
3 lbs. sugar
½ oz. citric acid (or 3 lemons, no pith, in lieu)
A pinch of grape tannin
Water to make up finally 1 gallon of must
Yeast nutrient and activated wine yeast

Method:

Scrub the beetroots. Slice thinly and boil in seven pints of water until tender (not mushy). Place the chopped figs, sugar and cloves into the initial fermentation vessel and strain into this the hot beetroot liquor. Stir well to dissolve sugar, etc. When cool (70°F.) add the citric acid, tannin and yeast nutrient. Introduce the activated yeast. Ferment on the "pulp" for 10 days, stirring every day and keeping the must closely covered. Then strain into fermentation vessel and ferment under protection of a fermentation lock in the usual manner. Rack in due course as necessary.

Beetroot and Cider

Ingredients:

   1 quart cider
   3–4 lbs. beetroot
   1 lb. raisins (or sultanas)
   ½ oz. citric acid (or 3 lemons, no pith, in lieu)
   A pinch of grape tannin
   3 lbs. sugar
   Water to make up finally 1 gallon of must
   Yeast nutrient and activated wine yeast

Method:

Scrub the beetroots and remove any green stalks. Slice thinly and boil in seven pints of water until tender (not mushy). Place the chopped raisins and sugar into the initial fermentation vessel and strain into this the hot beetroot liquor. Stir well with a wooden spoon to dissolve the sugar. When cool (70°F.) add the cider citric acid, grape tannin and yeast nutrient. Introduce the activated yeast and leave to ferment for 10 days closely covered, stirring the fermenting must daily with a wooden spoon. Then strain into fermentation jar and ferment under protection of a fermentation lock, racking in due course, as necessary.

Beetroot and Date

Ingredients:

   4 lbs. beetroot
   1 lb. malt extract
   1 lb. dates (or figs)
   3 lbs. sugar (or 4 lbs. invert sugar)
   ½ oz. citric acid (or 3 lemons, no pith, in lieu)
   $\frac{1}{10}$ oz. grape tannin (or ½ pint strong tea)
   Water to finally make up 1 gallon of must
   Yeast nutrient and activated wine yeast

Method:

Scrub the beetroots and remove any green stalks. Slice thinly and boil in seven pints of water until tender (avoid overboiling). Place the dates, sugar and malt extract into the initial fermentation vessel and strain into this hot beetroot liquor. Stir well with a wooden spoon to dissolve the sugar, etc. When cool (70°F.) add the citric acid, grape tannin and yeast nutrient. Introduce the activated wine yeast and ferment on the pulp for 10 days, stirring regularly with a wooden spoon, ensuring that the must is closely covered. Then strain into the secondary fermentation vessel and, leave to ferment under the protection of a fermentation lock racking as necessary in due course.

Beetroot and Prune

Ingredients:

> 3 lbs. beetroot
> 1 lb. prunes
> ½ bottle Vierka concentrated must (or 2 pints cider)
> 3 lbs. sugar (or 4 lbs. invert sugar)
> ½ oz. citric acid (or 3 lemons, no pith, in lieu)
> ½ pint strong tea (or ½ teaspoonful grape tannin)
> Water to finally make up 1 gallon of must
> Yeast nutrient and activated wine yeast

Method:

Scrub the beetroots and remove any green stalks. Slice thinly and boil in seven pints of water until tender (avoid overboiling) Place the chopped fruit and sugar into the initial fermentation vessel, and strain into this the hot beetroot liquor. Stir well with a wooden spoon to dissolve the sugar, etc. When cool (70°F.), add the citric acid, strong tea, Vierka must (or cider) and the yeast nutrient. Introduce the activated wine yeast and ferment on the pulp for 10 days, stirring each day with a wooden spoon and ensuring that the must is closely covered. Then strain into the secondary fermentation vessel and leave to ferment under the protection of a fermentation lock, racking as necessary in due course.

Bilberry (dried)

Ingredients:

> 1 lb. dried bilberries   1 gallon water
> ½ level teaspoon citric acid   Yeast and nutrient
> 2½ lbs. sugar

Method:

Bring the water to the boil and pour it over the bilberries and the sugar. Stir well to dissolve, adding the citric acid. Allow to cool to 70°F., then add the yeast and nutrient. Cover closely, and ferment in a warm place for seven days, stirring frequently to keep the "cap" of fruit wet and to prevent mould formation. Strain, then press the fruit and add this "run" to the other liquid. Put into fermentation jar and make up to one gallon if necessary with cold, boiled water. Do *not* throw the pulp away, but add to it a further gallon of boiling water, a further 2½ lbs. sugar, and fresh nutrient and yeast, and obtain a second batch of wine, lighter in colour but still worthwhile, from the same fruit. N.B.—Using this procedure, the addition of the fresh nutrient is all-important. Often a third, and even a fourth, gallon can be obtained in this way, each progressively fermented, and siphoned into a fermenting jar. One thus finishes up with two, three, or even four gallons of bilberry wine, all of different colour and body, and a year later it is possible to do some interesting blending to produce a red wine of exactly the type that one desires. Once in the fermenting jar, which should be opaque, or kept covered from the daylight to preserve the wine's glorious ruby colour, the wine is fermented, racked, and stored in the usual way. This is an easy wine to make in quantity, say five gallons at a time, if one has a large boiler.

Birch Sap

Ingredients:

1 gallon birch sap	3 lbs. white sugar
2 lemons	(or quart of honey)
1 sweet orange	1 Seville orange
½ lb. raisins	Yeast

Method:

Obtain a wooden beer or wine barrel tap, a piece of glass or plastic tubing, or even a piece of bamboo cane (with the pith removed). With a brace and bit of the same diameter bore a hole into the trunk of the tree just beyond the bark and insert the tap or tube, which should incline slightly downward to allow the sap to run easily. In March, when the sap is rising, it should be possible to draw off a gallon or so of liquor in two or three days. Plug the hole afterwards; if you do not the tree may die. Peel the oranges and lemons (no white pith) and boil in the sap for 20 minutes. Add enough water to restore the volume to the gallon, then pour into crock containing the sugar and chopped raisins. Stir until sugar is dissolved; when cool add the fruit juice and yeast. Cover the crock with a thick cloth and keep in a warm place until fermentation has quietened. Then strain into fermenting jar and fit trap.

Blackberry and Apple

Ingredients:

3 lbs. blackberries	Juice of two lemons
4 lbs. apples	1 gallon water
3 lbs. sugar	Yeast and nutrient

Method:

Chop the apples and put them with the blackberries and sugar into a bowl or plastic dustbin. Pour over them the water, boiling. Stir thoroughly. Allow to cool, then add the yeast nutrient, yeast and lemon juice.

Keep the vessel closely covered and stir the fruit each day to make sure that all is kept wet and no moulds form. Ferment on the pulp for a week, then strain into fermentation vessel and fit air lock. Ferment and rack into clean bottles when clear.

Blackcurrant

Ingredients:

3 lbs. blackcurrants	1 gallon water
3 lbs. preserving sugar	Yeast

Method:

Put the currants into a large earthenware jar and crush them. Boil up the sugar in the water and pour, still boiling, on to the currants. When it has cooled to about blood heat, add the yeast (wine yeast or a level teaspoonful of dried yeast) and keep closely covered for five days in a warm place, giving it an occasional stir. Then strain into a fermenting jar, and fit an air lock. Let it stand until fermentation ceases and the wine clears, usually in about three months, then siphon off into fresh, sterilised bottles.

Blackurrant and Raspberry

Ingredients:

3 lbs. blackcurrants
1 lb. raspberries
$\frac{1}{2}$ lb. malt extract
3 ozs. dried rose hips/shells
$\frac{1}{4}$ oz. citric acid (or 2 lemons, no pith, in lieu)
3 lbs. sugar
$\frac{1}{2}$ pint strong tea (or $\frac{1}{10}$ oz. grape tannin)
Yeast nutrient and activated wine yeast
Water: sufficient to finally produce 1 gallon of must

Method:

Remove the stalks, etc., from the fruits. Place these, together with the dried fruit, sugar and malt extract into the initial fermentation vessel. Pour in the boiling water, and stir well to dissolve the sugar and malt extract, and also to crush the fruit, use a wooden spoon. When cool, add the citric acid, strong tea, yeast nutrient and introduce the activated wine yeast. Cover securely and leave to ferment seven days, then strain into fermentation bottles. Fit air-lock and leave to ferment in the normal way, racking as necessary in due course. Avoid using mildewed and overripe berries.

As a variation:

Use 2 lbs. blackcurrants
1 lb. raspberries
1 lb. red currants or white currants
2 ozs. dried bananas instead of rose hips
1 lb. chopped raisins or sultanas instead of malt extract

Bramble Tip

Ingredients:

1 gallon bramble tips	1 gallon water
3 lbs. preserving sugar	Yeast

Method:

Place the tips in a crock and cover them with boiling water. Leave this to stand overnight, then bring to the boil and simmer gently for a quarter of an hour. Strain through muslin on to the sugar, add the yeast when it has cooled, and keep closely covered in a warm place for 10 days. Then pour into fermenting jar and fit trap. Leave until wine clears, then siphon off and bottle.

Broad Bean and Banana

Ingredients:

4 lbs. shelled broad beans
1 lb. bananas (or 2 ozs. dried variety)
$\frac{1}{2}$ lb. raisins or sultanas
$\frac{1}{2}$ pint strong tea (or $\frac{1}{10}$ oz. grape tannin)
1 level teaspoon citric acid (or 2 lemons, no pith, in lieu)
3 lbs. sugar (or 4 lbs. honey)
Yeast nutrient and activated wine yeast
Water: Sufficient to finally produce 1 gallon of "must"

Method:

Simmer gently the shelled beans in one gallon of water for one hour. Use only beans that are too old for culinary purposes and be sure that the skins do not break, otherwise there may be clearing difficulties. Place the chopped bananas, skins and raisins, together with the sugar, into the initial fermentation vessel. Pour in the broad bean liquor and stir well to dissolve the sugar. When cool add the strong tea, citric acid (and ½ oz. pectozyme if you wish), and yeast nutrient and introduce the activated wine yeast. Cover securely and leave to ferment for 10 days, stirring occasionally, then strain into secondary fermentation vessel. Fit airlock and leave to ferment in the normal way, racking later as necessary.

Celery and Apple

Ingredients:

3 lbs. celery (green portions included)
3 lbs. cooking apples (or 1 quart cider)
½ pint grape concentrate
3 lbs. sugar
¼ oz. tartaric acid (B.P. quality)
¼ oz. ammonium phosphate (B.P. quality)
Water to make up 1 gallon of "must"
Activated wine yeast

Method:

Thinly slice the celery and grate the cooking apples, including cores and skins. Place these together with the sugar into the initial fermentation vessel. Pour on the *boiling* water and stir with a wooden spoon to dissolve the sugar, etc. When cool add the grape concentrate (or cider), tartaric acid and ammonium phosphate, introduce the activated wine yeast and ferment on the "pulp" for 10 days, stirring the "must" with a wooden spoon twice daily, ensuring that the "must" is closely covered. Then strain, for secondary fermentation, into fermentation vessel, and fit air lock. Leave to ferment in the normal way, racking as necessary in due course.

Charlock

The bright yellow flowers of the charlock or wild mustard can be seen in the cornfields from May to August. It is a nuisance to the farmer among the corn in its early stages, but an excellent wine can be made from its flowers and leaves.

26

Ingredients:

    1 gallon charlock flowers and leaves (no stalks)
    3½ lbs. sugar
    ½ pint cold tea
    2 lemons (or 1 level teaspoon citric acid)
    1 lb. crushed barley, maize or rice
    1 gallon water
    Activated yeast and nutrient

Method:

    Place the flowers and bruised leaves of the charlock together with the crushed barley, maize or rice. Grated lemon rinds (no pith) and sugar in the fermentation vessel. Add *boiling* water and stir to dissolve the sugar then leave to cool. Add the cold tea, lemon juice or citric acid, activated yeast and nutrient. Ferment and rack in the usual way.

Cherry

Ingredients:

    8 lbs. black cherries (weighed whole and then stoned)
    7 pints water
    1 Campden tablet
    3½ lbs. granulated sugar
    Yeast and nutrient

Method:

    Wash fruit well. Crush it with a wooden spoon in a bowl. Bring four pints of the water to the boil and pour it over fruit. Crush the Campden tablet and mix it into two tablespoons warm water; stir it into fruit. Allow to stand for two hours. Boil remaining water and dissolve sugar in it. Pour sugar and water over fruit and stir well. Allow mixture to cool slightly, then add yeast. Cover the bowl with polythene and leave in a warm place for seven days for the first fermentation. Then strain mixture through muslin or nylon sieve into gallon jar. Discard "pulp." Plug jar with cork and lock, and leave to ferment. When second fermentation has ceased, rack the wine and siphon it into bottles.

Cherry and Red-currant

Ingredients:

    6–8 lbs. cherries (any colour)
    1 lb. red currants
    2 ozs. dried bananas or 3 ozs. dried rose hips/shells
    ½ lb. malt extract
    ⅜ oz. citric acid (or 1 lemon, no pith, in lieu)
    ¼ pint strong tea or a small pinch of grape tannin
    3 lbs. sugar or 4 lbs. honey
    Yeast nutrient and activated wine yeast
    Water: sufficient to produce finally 1 gallon of "must"

Method:

Macerate the fruits, ensuring no stalks are used, and remove the stones. Either the stones may now be discarded or the stones may be cracked (as in France) and placed in the "must." Add the dried fruits and malt extract and sugar, then pour in the hot water and stir to dissolve the sugar. When cool add the acid, strong tea, yeast nutrient and introduce the activated wine yeast. Cover closely and leave to ferment seven days (a Campden tablet may be used initially if desired); then strain into the fermentation bottle and leave to ferment in the normal way after fitting airlock, racking as necessary in due course.

Variation:

1. A quart of cider may be used in lieu of the dried fruits.
2. Use paddy rice with husks, barley or wheat grains in lieu of dried fruits.

Citrus

Ingredients:

12 oranges	
6 Seville oranges	**This quantity for**
4 tangerines	**4 gallons.**
6 grapefruit	**Reduce proportionately**
12 lemons	**for lesser quantities.**
1 lb. sultanas	
10 lb. sugar *will give the sweetness of a Sauternes*	

Method:

Squeeze juice of all fruit into crock or polythene dustbin and add sultanas and 1 gallon of water. Pare very thinly the skins of a quarter of the fruit (no white pith) and pour on them 1 quart of *boiling* water. When cool add liquid to the tub containing the juice and throw the skins on the compost heap, add water to make up to two gallons and yeast and 5 lbs. of the sugar. Cover closely and leave for two weeks, stirring daily. Then add another two gallons of water and the rest of the sugar and leave until vigorous fermentation quietens down; rack off and put into casks or jars, fit airlock and proceed in the usual manner. Since Seville oranges and tangerines can be obtained only in January or February, two extra sweet oranges and two tablespoonsful of marmalade may be substituted. Sugar may be added in stages and quantities according to the individual's usual practice.

"I wish you'd let it ferment out BEFORE you drink it"

Comfrey

Ingredients:

5 Comfrey roots
1 pint strong cold tea
2 lbs. apples or 1 pint cider
4 lbs. sugar (or 3 lbs. sugar and 1 lb. chopped raisins)

2 lemons or citric acid
2 oranges
Yeast nutrient
Yeast (selected wine)

Method:

Dig up and prepare by washing, peeling and cutting into fairly small pieces five Comfrey roots. Boil these in one gallon of water until tender, skim and strain on to the sugar, then add the grated apple or cider, the cold strong tea, lemon juice or citric acid. Orange juice and juice from the boiled lemon and orange peel (no pith). When cool stir in the yeast nutrient and selected wine yeast. Ferment on the "solids" for five days, then strain into fermentation jar, fit air-lock and ferment in normal way.

Concentrate (white)

Ingredients:

½ gallon Hidalgo grape concentrate (S.G. 1.400)
3 gallons water
1 oz. tartaric acid
1 lb. dried apricots (chopped)

2 Campden tablets
3 lbs. white sugar
1 lb. Barbados sugar
1 lb. glucose
1 large Bramley apple

Method:

Mix ½ gallon Hidalgo's 1.400 grape concentrate with the water, tartaric acid, all the sugar and glucose, 8 ozs. dried apricots (chopped) and Campden tablets. Set aside to ferment with a good wine yeast (or Hidalgo's dry wine yeast compound), air-lock is optional but keep well covered. After about 10 days when fermentation is well proceeding MIX INTO THE FERMENTING BREW one large Bramley apple and ½ lb. dried apricots, both previously pulped, then continue the fermentation process in the usual way. Ferment on the "pulp" for at least another 10 days, then strain. The above brew can be prepared from RED or WHITE CONCENTRATE. Variations may be made by adding to the fermenting brew, at any stage, 3–4 lbs. of prepared GOOSEBERRIES, BLACK-CURRANTS/BERRIES, PLUMS, RASPBERRIES, SLOES, PRUNES, PEACHES.

Concentrate (red)

Ingredients:

1 quart Hidalgo red Tintorero concentrate
1 lb. dried elderberries (or bilberries)
4 oranges (juice and pulp only, no peel)
1¼ oz. citric acid
1 teaspoon grape tannin
4 teaspoons yeast nutrient
8–9 lbs. sugar
4 gallons water

Method:

Add near boiling water to all the above (suggest fruit in a nylon bag and use of a plastic dustbin); stir to dissolve the sugar, cover until cool. Add a working all-purpose wine yeast starter, fermenting 7–10 days, remove fruit and drain, rack the "must" in to a container, fit an air-lock and allow to work out—about one month—then rack.

Cowslip

Ingredients:

1 gallon cowslip flower heads	Yeast
1 gallon cold water	Yeast nutrient
3 lbs. preserving sugar	Pinch of isinglass

Method:

Use all the heads, but not the main stalks, and pour the water over the flowers. Leave to soak for seven days, stirring daily, so that the flowers infuse thoroughly. Then squeeze the flowers out. Pour the liquid over the sugar, and add yeast nutrient, yeast, and a pinch of isinglass, and put in a warm place, closely covered, to ferment. After 14 days skim and place into fermenting bottle, and fit trap. Bottle finally when the wine clears. At a year old this is a strong, delicately-flavoured wine.

Crab Apple

Ingredients:

1 gallon crab apples	Yeast
3½ lbs. sugar	Nutrient
1 lb. raisins	1 gallon boiling water

Method:

Crush the crab apples in a bowl or tub and pour the *boiling* water over them. Stir and mash for 10 days, then strain. If you have a press, press the "pulp" and add the resulting juice to the rest. Stir the sugar in to the liquid and add the chopped raisins and yeast and nutrient. Cover the bowl closely and stand it in a warm place for 14 days for the initial fermentation then strain into a fermenting jar and fit a fermentation lock. Rack into clean bottles when it is clear and the fermentation is complete.

Cups

CIDER CUP

Ingredients:

1 pint cider	Ginger and nutmeg
1 pint ale or beer	1 wineglass gin or whisky
Treacle or sugar	

Method:

Heat up the cider and ale and sweeten to taste with the sugar or treacle, then grate in ginger and nutmeg. Add gin or whisky and serve piping hot.

KENTISH CUP

Ingredients:

½ pint sherry or fortified country wine	2 oranges
	1 lemon
1 quart sweet cider or sweet white wine	Angostura bitters

Method:

Put the finely grated rind of an orange in a punch bowl or jug. Add ½ pint sherry, cover and stand for half an hour. Add the sweet cider (or any sweet white wine) and the juice of one orange and of a lemon. Stir and sweeten to taste. Just before serving add a thinly sliced orange and two teaspoons Angostura Aromatic Bitters. Serve chilled.

SUMMER CUP

Here is a novel "cup" for summer parties:

Ingredients:

1 bottle red or white wine	2–3 lumps sugar
1 glass sherry	1 lemon
2 bottles soda water	A sprig of borage

Method:

Chill the bottles of wine and soda water. Thinly pare the lemon rinds (no pith) and rub the rinds on to the sugar to remove the zest. Fifteen minutes before serving pour the chilled soda water and wine into a large jug, add lemon juice from half a lemon, the lemon flavoured sugar and the sherry. Add a little powdered sugar to taste and add the borage.

The flavour and strength will be agreeably varied if a liqueur glass of orange Curacao and a few slices of orange are added. The amount of soda water may be reduced to give another variation. Avoid using ice in the jug; the bottle of wine must be chilled thoroughly. If only ice is available, stand the jug in the ice. Strips of cucumber may be used in lieu of borage.

APPLE CUP

Ingredients:

> 1 bottle (26 ozs.) apple wine
> 3 bottles (78 ozs.) grape wine or 4 bottles any good brew
> 16 ozs. S.A. medium dry sherry
> 24 ozs. old English cider
> 10 ozs. brandy

Method:

Why not try this recipe for a wine cup contrived by Lieut.-Col. D. M. FitzGerald, of Five Chimneys, Friday Street, Eyke? He writes: I used one part apple to three parts red grape merely because that was what I had available. The colour was excellent and it looked good served out of a punch bowl (borrowed from the local wine merchant, no charge!) with mint and sliced lemon and peel floating in it. This should be sufficient for 40 claret glasses. The effect was excellent! It should be noted that all the ingredients are alcoholic. If something less potent is required tonic water, etc., could be used instead of, or as well as, cider.

PINEAPPLE COOLER (To make 40 wine glasses)

Ingredients:

½ pint strong tea	8 ozs. sugar
¼ pint lemon juice	1 tin pineapple slices
¾ pint orange juice	4 1-pint bottles ginger
2 tablespoons lime juice cordial	4 1-pint bottles soda

Method:

Place tea, fruit juices, cordial and sugar in bowl. Put on ice or in cool place to chill. Just before serving add pineapple slices and juice, ginger ale and soda water.

Dandelion

Ingredients:

2 quarts dandelion heads
2½ lbs. preserving sugar
  (3 lbs. if a sweet wine
  is desired)

4 oranges
1 gallon water
Yeast and nutrient

Method:

Pick the flowers when the sun is on them and they are fully open. Use the whole head (but no stem) and do not bother to pick off the individual petals, which is an exasperating and unnecessary chore. Pour the *boiling* water over the flowers and leave for two days. Boil the mixture for 10 minutes with the orange peel (no white pith) and strain through muslin on to the sugar. When cool add the fruit juice, yeast and yeast nutrient. Keep in a warm place, closely covered, for four days, then pour into fermenting jar and fit trap. Leave till it clears, then siphon off into clean bottles. This makes an excellent white table wine.

Dandelion and Burdock

Ingredients:

¼ lb. dandelion leaves
¼ lb. burdock leaves and burrs
5 quarts water

4 lbs. sugar
2 lbs. rice

Method:

Boil the dandelion and burdock together in the water for 40 minutes, then strain on to the rice and sugar. When cool, add yeast and the juice of a lemon and cover closely. Stir each day for eight days, then strain into fermenting jar and fit trap. Rack into bottles when clear.

Dandelion and Raisin

Ingredients:

2–3 quarts flower heads (without calyx)
1 lb. stoned raisins (or mixed dried fruit)
3 lbs. sugar
½ oz. citric acid (or 3 lemons, no pith, in lieu)
½ pint cold strong tea (or a pinch of Grape Tannin)
7½ pints water
Yeast nutrient and activated wine yeast

Method:

Discard as much as possible of the green portion of the flower (without being too fussy about it). Then measure the yellow heads and place these in a crock pouring over them $7\frac{1}{2}$ pints of *boiling* water. Cover the crock well and leave to soak for two days. Do not exceed this period otherwise harmful moulds may grow. Transfer the flower heads and resulting liquor to a boiler and bring to boiling point only. Meanwhile place the sugar and dried fruit into the initial fermentation vessel and strain on to the sugar, etc., the liquor from the flower heads and stir to dissolve the sugar. When cool add the strong tea, citric acid, yeast nutrient and introduce the activated wine yeast. Ferment on the "pulp" for 10 days, then siphon into fermentation jar making up the "must" to one gallon necessary. Fit air-lock and ferment to a finish in the normal way, racking as necessary in due course.

Dandelion and Ginger

Ingredients:

1 lb. or 2–3 quarts of flower heads
$\frac{1}{2}$ oz. essence cayenne
$\frac{1}{2}$ oz. essence ginger
1 pint cold strong tea
$\frac{1}{2}$ oz. tartaric acid
3 lbs. sugar
$7\frac{1}{2}$ pints water
Yeast nutrient and activated wine yeast

Method:

The whole heads can be used in this recipe if desired. Place the flower heads in a boiler, add the water and bring to *boiling* point only. Cut off heat and leave to infuse, as for tea, for one hour. Bring the liquor and heads back to *boiling* point only and strain the liquor on to the cayenne, ginger and sugar which has been placed into the initial fermentation vessel. Stir until sugar is dissolved. When cool add strong tea, tartaric acid, yeast nutrient and activated wine yeast. Fit air-lock and ferment in the normal way, racking if necessary.

Dandelion and Rice

Ingredients:

2–3 quarts of flower heads (without calyx)
2 lbs. paddy rice (with husk)
1 lb. stoned raisins (or mixed dried fruit)
3 lbs. sugar
½ oz. citric acid (or 3 lemons, no pith, in lieu)
½ pint cold strong tea (or a pinch of grape tannin)
7½ pints water
Yeast nutrient and activated wine yeast

Method:

Prepare and measure the flower heads, discarding as much as possible of the green part of the flower head. Place flower heads in polythene bucket or crock and pour over them 7½ pints *boiling* water. Cover the vessel well and leave to soak for 48 hours (no longer). Transfer the flower heads and liquor into a saucepan or boiler and bring to *boiling* point only. Place the sugar, paddy rice and raisins into the initial fermentation vessel then pour in the strained flower head liquor and stir to dissolve the sugar. When cool add the cold strong tea, citric acid, yeast nutrient and introduce the activated wine yeast; ferment on the "pulp" for 10 days Then siphon into fermentation jar, making up to one gallon if necessary. Fit air-lock and ferment to a finish in the normal way. Rack as necessary in due course.

Dandelion and Rosehip

Ingredients:

2–3 quarts of flower heads (without calyx)
8 ozs. dried rose hips or
4 ozs. rose hip/shells (a handful of dried elderberries or bilberries
    will give this wine an excellent colour)
3½ lbs. sugar
½ oz. citric acid (or 3 lemons, no pith, in lieu)
½ pint cold strong tea (or a pinch of grape tannin)
7½ pints water
Yeast nutrient and activated wine yeast

Method:

Measure the flower heads from which almost all the green portion has been removed. Place the flower heads in a crock or plastic vessel and cover with 7½ pints of *boiling* water and cover well, leaving to soak for 48 hours (no longer). Transfer the flowers and liquor to a boiler or saucepan and heat to *boiling* point only. Place the sugar and rose hips into the initial fermentation vessel and strain on to these the liquor from the flower heads. Stir to dissolve the sugar. When cool add the strong tea, citric acid, yeast nutrient and introduce the activated wine yeast. Ferment on the "pulp" for 10 days (1 lb. dried fruit can be added with advantage). Then siphon into fermentation jar making up the "must" to one gallon if necessary. Fit air-lock and ferment to a finish in the normal way, racking as necessary in due course.

Dandelion and Date

Ingredients:

2–3 quarts of flower heads (without calyx)
2 lbs. dried figs
3 lbs. sugar
½ oz. citric acid (or 3 lemons, no pith, in lieu)
½ pint cold strong tea (or a pinch of grape tannin)
7½ pints water
Yeast nutrient and activated wine yeast

Method:

Prepare and measure the flower heads, if you prefer to work in terms of weight up to 1 lb. of prepared flower heads may be used. Bring the water to *boiling* point and add the flower heads. Leave for one hour to infuse as in tea making, then bring liquor up to *boiling* point once again, and strain this liquor on to the chopped figs and sugar which have been placed into the initial fermentation vessel, and stir to dissolve the sugar. When cool add the strong tea, citric acid, yeast nutrient and introduce the activated wine yeast. Ferment on the "pulp" for 10 days, then siphon into fermentation jar making up the "must" to one gallon if necessary. Fit air lock and ferment to a finish in the normal way, racking as necessary in due course.

Dandelion and Prune

Ingredients:

2–3 quarts flower heads
1 lb. prunes (other dried fruits can be used, in lieu)
1 lb. honey (if available)
¼ bottle Vierka Concentrated Wine Must
2½ lbs. sugar (use 3 lbs. of sugar if honey is not used)
1 pint cold strong tea
½ oz. citric acid (or 3 lemons, no pith, in lieu)
7½ pints of water
Yeast nutrient and activated wine yeast

Method:

Place the whole heads in a boiler, add water and bring to *boiling* point only. Cut off the heat and leave to infuse for one hour (as for making tea). Bring the liquor with flower heads back to *boiling* point only, then strain this liquor on to the chopped prunes and sugar in the initial fermentation vessel. Stir well to dissolve sugar. When lukewarm stir in honey and leave to cool, then add Concentrated Wine Must, strong tea, citric acid, yeast nutrient and activated wine yeast. Keep well covered for 10 days, then siphon into fermentation jar, air-lock, and ferment to a finish in the normal way, rack as necessary in due course.

Date (dry)

Ingredients:

4 lbs. dates	Juice of 4 lemons
½ lb. Demerara sugar	Yeast and nutrient

Method:

The dates should be chopped and slowly boiled with half a pound of Demerara sugar in one gallon of water for half an hour. Ample sugar will then have been extracted from them. It helps to add a few date stones during the boiling to impart a very slight bitterness to give the wine zest.

When the liquid has cooled, strain, and add the rind and juice, the lemons, the yeast and yeast nutrient, and ferment under an air lock in the usual way. When the wine fully clears, rack and mature for six months. This is best made as a sweet dessert wine and the fermentation can often be prolonged by "feeding" with small doses of sugar, adding 4 ozs. each time the S.G. has dropped to 1.000.

Date (sweet)

(Medium sweet, Cream Sherry type wine)

Ingredients:

4 lbs. dates
2 lbs. sugar
1 gallon water
1 grapefruit

2 large lemons
1 orange
Sherry yeast and nutrient

Method:

Chop and boil the dates gently for half an hour with the rinds of the fruit (leave half a dozen of the date stones in the saucepan but omit the others). Strain on to the sugar, add the fruit juice, and stir well to dissolve. When cool add the yeast and nutrient, put into fermentation jar and fit trap. Ferment out, adding sugar in 4 oz. lots towards the end of the fermentation, as necessary, each time gravity reaches 1.000.

Elderberry (dried)

Ingredients:

½ lb. dried elderberries
1 lb. of raisins
1 good teaspoonful of citric acid
3 lbs. sugar
1 H.F. nutrient
A Vierka liquid, port, Bordeaux or Burgundy yeast (whichever character wine you may desire)

Method:

Place the elderberries and sugar in a polythene bucket. Pour on a gallon of *boiling* water. Allow to cool (75°F.) add the yeast, nutrient and citric acid. Allow to ferment for one week. Strain into a gallon jar with fermentation lock. Fermentation will be complete in 6–7 weeks. Rack into bottles and stopper lightly with cotton wool for 2–3 weeks. Then cork. This is one of the finest red wines that the amateur winemaker can make and compares most favourably with good claret. For other wines the elderberries can be replaced with bilberries, rowan berries, or sloes, all of which will give excellent results.

Elderberry Enchant

Ingredients:

3 lbs. elderberries (or 3–4 lbs. dried elderberries)
1½ pints grape juice concentrate (or 4 lbs. or more fresh grapes)
1 lb. cornflour (also known as yellow cornmeal)
2½ lbs. sugar (or 3 lbs. honey)
2 ozs. crushed barley (wheat or wholemeal rice)
½ pint strong tea
½ oz. tartaric acid
 ½ oz. citric acid
¼ oz. ammonium phosphate
Water to finally make up 1 gallon of "must"
Yeast nutrient and activated wine yeast

Method:

Place the berries, cornflower, sugar and grains into the initial fermentation vessel. Pour in the *boiling* water, macerate the fruits and stir well with a wooden spoon to break up the berries and dissolve the sugar. When cool, add the grape concentrate, tartaric and citric acid, tea, ammonium phosphate, and yeast nutrient. Introduce the activated wine yeast and ferment on the "pulp" for 10 days, stirring the "must" twice daily with a wooden spoon and keep closely covered. Then strain, for secondary fermentation, into fermentation vessel and fit air-lock. Leave to ferment in the normal way, racking as necessary in due course.

Elderberry and Apricot (dry, red)

Ingredients:

½ pint elderflowers (or a small packet of dried flowers)
1 lb. dried apricots or peaches (2 lbs. may be used if desired)
4 ozs. dried bananas (or 2 lbs. fresh bananas)
1 lb. raisins or sultanas (or ½ pint white grape concentrate may be used instead)
½ pint strong tea or ¼ teaspoonful grape tannin
½ oz. tartaric/citric acid mixed, i.e., ¼ oz. each
1 oz. glycerine (B.P. quality)
3 lbs. sugar
Yeast nutrient and activated (Sauternes) wine yeast
Sufficient water to finally produce 1 gallon of "must"

Method

Prepare the flower heads, chop the fruits and place these together with the sugar into the initial fermentation vessel. Pour in *boiling* water and stir to dissolve the sugar. When cool add the strong tea, acids, glycerine, yeast nutrient and introduce the activated yeast. Cover well, and leave to ferment for 10 days, then siphon into fermentation bottles and fit air lock. Leave to ferment in the normal way, racking later as necessary in due course. The flower heads should be gathered on a fine day and use only those in full bloom. If dried elderflower and dried fruits are used, elderflower wine can be made all the year round.

Elderberry and Beetroot (med. sweet)

Ingredients:

3 lbs. elderberries (or $\frac{3}{4}$ lb. dried elderberries)
2 lbs. beetroot (or sugar beet)
1 lb. raisins (or 1 lb. figs, dates, sultanas, currants, etc.)
2 ozs. dried bananas (or 1 lb. bananas including skins)
3 lbs. sugar (or 4 lbs. honey)
$\frac{1}{2}$ oz. citric acid (or 3 lemons, no pith, in lieu)
$\frac{1}{2}$ pint strong tea (or a pinch of grape tannin)
$\frac{1}{4}$ oz. pectozyme
Water to finally make up 1 gallon of "must"
Yeast nutrient and activated wine yeast

Method:

Wash the beetroot, do not peel, slice up thinly and boil in water until tender, but not mushy. Place the elderberries and chopped dried fruits together with the sugar into the initial fermentation vessel and strain on to these the *boiling* beetroot liquor. Stir well with a wooden spoon to break up the berries and to dissolve the sugar. When cool add the citric acid, strong tea, pectozyme and yeast nutrient. Introduce the activated wine yeast and ferment on the "pulp" for 10 days, stirring the "must" twice daily with a wooden spoon. Then strain for secondary fermentation, into fermentation vessel and fit air-lock. Leave to ferment in the normal way, racking as necessary in due course.

Elderberry and Carrot (dry, red)

Ingredients:

2 lbs. elderberries
2 lbs. carrots
1 lb. malt extract
2 lbs. sugar
1 level teaspoon citric acid
Water to finally make up 1 gallon of "must"
Yeast nutrient and activated wine yeast

Method:

Scrub and thinly slice the carrots and place these in a saucepan containing *boiling* water and simmer for 10 minutes, then place the berries, malt extract and sugar into the initial fermentation vessel and pour over these the carrots and *boiling* carrot liquor. Stir well with a wooden spoon to break up the berries and to dissolve the malt extract and sugar. When cool, add the acid and yeast nutrient. Introduce the activated wine yeast and ferment on the "pulp" for 10 days, stirring the "must" twice daily with a wooden spoon. Then strain, for secondary fermentation, into fermentation vessel and fit air-lock. Leave to ferment in the normal way, racking as necessary in due course.

Elderberry and Red Gooseberry

Ingredients:

2 lbs. Elderberries (or ½ lb. dried elderberries)

1 lb. red gooseberries (or blackberries/loganberries, etc.)

1 lb. raisins (or mixed dried fruit, currants, sultanas, etc.)

3 lbs. sugar (or 4 lbs. honey)

1 level teaspoon citric acid (or 3 lemons, no pith, in lieu)

¼ oz. pectozyme

Water to finally make up 1 gallon of "must"

Yeast nutrient and activated wine yeast

Method:

Macerate the fruits and place these together with the chopped dried fruits and sugar into the initial fermentation vessel. Pour in the *boiling* water and stir well with a wooden spoon to dissolve the sugar. When cool, add the acid, pectozyme, and yeast nutrient. Introduce the activated wine yeast and ferment on the "pulp" for 10 days, stirring the must twice daily with a wooden spoon and keep closely covered. Then strain, for secondary fermentation, into fermentation vessel and fit air-lock. Leave to ferment in the normal way, racking as necessary in due course.

Elderberry and Hawthornberry (medium)

Ingredients:

> 3 lbs. elderberries (or ¾ lb. dried elderberries)
> 2 lbs. hawthornberries (or ½ lb. dried bilberries or rowanberries)
> 1 lb. wholemeal rice (crushed maize, barley or wheat may be substituted)
> 1 lb. raisins (or sultanas, figs, currants, etc.)
> 3 lbs. sugar (or 4 lbs. honey)
> ½ oz. citric acid (or 3 lemons, no pith, in lieu)
> ½ pint strong tea (or a pinch of grape tannin)
> ½ oz. pectozyme
>
> Water to finally make up 1 gallon of "must"
> Yeast nutrient and activated wine yeast

Method:

Place the berries, grains, chopped dried fruits, and sugar into the initial fermentation vessel. Pour in the *boiling* water. Macerate the fruits and stir well with a wooden spoon to break up the fruits and dissolve the sugar. When cool add the acid, strong tea, pectozyme and yeast nutrient. Introduce the activated wine yeast and ferment on the "pulp" for 10 days, stirring the "must" twice daily with a wooden spoon and keep closely covered. Then strain, for secondary fermentation, into fermentation vessel and fit air-lock. Leave to ferment in the normal way, racking as necessary in due course.

Elderberry and Huckleberry (sweet)

Ingredients:

> 2 lbs. elderberries
> 2 lbs. *huckleberries
> 2 ozs. dried bananas
> 3 lbs. sugar
> 1 level teaspoon citric acid
> ¼ oz. pectozyme
>
> Water to finally make up 1 gallon of "must"
> Yeast nutrient and activated wine yeast

*Only the garden huckleberry, "Solanum Nigrum Var. Guinense" should be used—other varieties may prove inedible.

Method:

Place the berries and dried fruit into the initial fermentation vessel. Pour in the *boiling* water. Macerate the fruits and stir well with a wooden spoon to break up the berries and dissolve the sugar. When cool, add the acid, pectozyme and yeast nutrient. Introduce the activated wine yeast and ferment on the "pulp" for 10 days, stirring the "must" twice daily with a wooden spoon and keep closely covered. Then strain, for secondary fermentation, into fermentation vessel and fit air-lock. Leave to ferment in the normal way, racking as necessary in due course.

Elderberry and Marrow

Ingredients:

3 lbs. elderberries (or $\frac{3}{4}$ lb. dried elderberries)
5 lbs. ripe marrow (or melon)
1 lb. malt extract (or $\frac{1}{4}$ bottle Vierka Concentrated Must)
3 lbs. sugar (or 4 lbs. honey)
$\frac{1}{2}$ oz. citric acid (or 3 lemons, no pith, in lieu)
$\frac{1}{2}$ pint strong tea (or a pinch of grape tannin)
$\frac{1}{4}$ oz. pectozyme

Water to finally make up 1 gallon of "must"
Yeast nutrient and activated wine yeast

Method:

Place the berries and shredded marrow (including skin and seeds) together with the malt extract and sugar into the initial fermentation vessel. (If Vierka "must" is used, add when "must" is cool.) Pour in the *boiling* water. Macerate the fruits and stir well with a wooden spoon to break up the fruits and to dissolve the sugar. When cool, add the citric acid, strong tea, pectozyme and yeast nutrient. Introduce the activated wine yeast and ferment on the "pulp" for 10 days, stirring the "must" twice daily with a wooden spoon, and keep closely covered. Then strain, for secondary fermentation, into fermentation vessel and fit air-lock. Leave to ferment in the normal way, racking as necessary in due course.

Elderberry and Pear

Ingredients:

3 lbs. elderberries (or $\frac{3}{4}$ lb. dried elderberries)
3 lbs. ripe pears (or 3 lbs. mixed apples or 1 lb. dried apples / pears)
1 lb. raisins (or mixed dried fruit, currants, sultanas, etc.)
3 lbs. sugar (or 4 lbs. honey)
$\frac{1}{4}$ oz. citric acid (or 3 lemons, no pith, in lieu)
$\frac{1}{4}$ pint strong tea (or a pinch of grape tannin)
$\frac{1}{2}$ oz. pectozyme

Water to finally make up 1 gallon of "must"
Yeast nutrient and activated wine yeast

Method:

Place the elderberries, shredded pears, dried fruit and sugar into the initial fermentation vessel. Pour in the *boiling* water, and stir well with a wooden spoon to break up the fruits and to dissolve the sugar. When cool, add the citric acid, strong tea, pectozyme and yeast nutrient. Introduce the activated wine yeast and ferment on the "pulp" for 10 days, stirring the "must" twice daily with a wooden spoon and keep closely covered. Then strain, for secondary fermentation, into fermentation vessel, and fit air-lock. Leave to ferment in the normal way, racking as necessary in due course.

Elderberry and Raisin

Ingredients:

3 lbs. elderberries	½ oz. of citric acid
1 lb. raisins	Yeast and nutrients
3 lbs. sugar	

Method:

Strip the berries from the stalks and whilst you are doing this bring one gallon of water to the boil. Put the elderberries in a bowl and crush them and add the chopped or minced raisins. Then pour over them the *boiling* water, allow to cool to 70°F. before adding the yeast, acid and nutrient. Cover closely and leave for three days in a warm place, stirring daily, then strain through a nylon sieve on to the sugar. Pour the liquor into a gray hen or stone jar or a dark glass bottle (in clear glass the wine will lose its glorious ruby colour) but do not fill completely until the first vigorous ferment has subsided. When it has top up with spare liquor or cold boiled water and fit fermentation lock. Leave till fermentation is complete then syphon off into clean, dark bottles. If you have no dark ones cover your white ones with a sugar bag or brown paper, or keep them in a dark cupboard. You will find that this makes an excellent wine.

Elderflower (light, sweet)

Ingredients:

½ pint elderflowers	1 orange
3 lbs. preserving sugar	Yeast
1 gallon water	Yeast nutrient
2 lemons	

Method:

The flowers should be gathered on a sunny day when in full bloom and the florets be cut or removed from the main green stalks. One needs enough to half fill a pint jug, not pressed down. Put the flowerlets into a crock, with the lemon rinds (no white pith) and the sugar and pour the *boiling* water on to them. Stir to dissolve the sugar, and leave until cool; then add the yeast, yeast nutrient, and lemon juice. Leave closely covered in a warm place for four days, then strain into fermenting jar and fit air-lock. Leave until it clears and fermentation has ceased; then siphon off into clean bottles. A clean-tasting, appetising wine.

Elderflower Champagne

Ingredients:

$\frac{1}{4}$ pint flower heads (2 flowerheads)
$1\frac{1}{2}$ lbs. sugar
1 teaspoonful citric acid (or 1 lemon, no pith)
$\frac{1}{4}$ pint strong tea
Yeast

Method:

Pour $\frac{1}{2}$ gallon *boiling* water over the prepared flower heads and leave well covered to soak for 24 hours, to infuse as in making tea. Then bring to *boiling* point and strain on to the sugar in the initial fermentation vessel. Stir well to dissolve the sugar. When cool add $\frac{1}{2}$ gal. cold water, acid, tea and yeast, cover well and leave to ferment for seven days. Then siphon into screw topped cider or flagon bottles and keep for 14–21 days when it is ready to drink. When opening the bottles pour off into a glass (half pint or so), then, without righting the bottle pour the remainder into another screw-top bottle thus ensuring the maximum of clear brew. Do not exceed the quantity of blooms or sugar stated and prepare and drink as for "Home Brew."

Elderflower and Apricot

Ingredients:

$\frac{1}{2}$ pint elderflowers (or a small packet of dried flowers)
1 lb. dried apricots or peaches (2 lbs. may be used if desired)
4 ozs. dried bananas (or 2 lbs. fresh bananas)
1 lb. raisins or sultanas (or $\frac{1}{2}$ pint white grape concentrate may be used instead)
$\frac{1}{2}$ pint strong tea (or $\frac{1}{4}$ teaspoonful grape tannin)
$\frac{1}{2}$ oz. tartaric/citric acid mixed, i.e., $\frac{1}{4}$ oz. each
1 oz. glycerine (B.P. quality)
3 lbs. sugar

Method:

Yeast nutrient and activated (Sauternes) wine yeast sufficient to finally produce 1 gallon of "must"

Prepare the flower heads, chop the fruits and place these together with the sugar into the initial fermentation vessel. Pour in *boiling* water and stir to dissolve the sugar. When cool add the strong tea, acids, glycerine, yeast nutrient and introduce the activated yeast. Cover well, and leave to ferment for 10 days, then siphon into fermentation bottles and fit air-lock. Leave to ferment in the normal way, racking later as necessary in due course. The flower heads should be gathered on a fine day and use only those in full bloom. If dried elderflower and dried fruits are used, elderflower wine can be made all the year round.

Elderflower and Carrot

Ingredients:

½ pint elderflowers (or a small packet of dried flowers)

3 lbs. young carrots (young turnips or swedes can be substituted)

1 lb. raisins/sultanas or figs

½ oz. citric acid (or 3 lemons, no pith, in lieu)

½ pint strong tea (or ¼ teaspoonful grape tannin)

3 lbs. sugar

Yeast nutrient and activated wine yeast

Sufficient water to finally produce 1 gallon of "must"

Method:

Scrub the young carrots and slice thinly. Boil the carrots until they are *just tender*. Place the prepared flowers, chopped fruit, and sugar into the initial fermentation vessel and strain over these, the *boiling* carrot extract. Stir well to dissolve the sugar. When cool add the acid, strong tea, yeast nutrient and introduce the activated wine yeast. Cover well and leave to ferment for 10 days. Then siphon into fermentation bottles and fit air-lock. Leave to ferment in normal way, racking later as necessary. The delicate, fragrant and wholly delectable elderflower wine can only be produced by using flower heads of full bloom, otherwise a bitter taste may be imparted to the wine.

Elderflower and Cider

Ingredients:

$\frac{1}{2}$ pint elderflowers (or a small packet of dried flowers)
1 quart bottle commercial, draught or home-made cider (or $\frac{1}{4}$ bottle Vierka Concentrated Must)
1 lb. raisins or sultanas
$\frac{1}{2}$ oz. citric acid (or 3 lemons, no pith, in lieu)
$\frac{1}{4}$ pint strong tea (or $\frac{1}{4}$ teaspoonful grape tannin)
3 lbs. sugar

Yeast nutrient and activated wine yeast
Sufficient water to finally produce 1 gallon "must"

Method:

Prepare the elderflowers and place these with the chopped fruit and sugar in the initial fermentation vessel and pour over the *boiling* water and stir well to dissolve the sugar. When cool add the juice of the lemons, strong tea and yeast nutrient, and introduce the activated wine yeast. Cover well and leave to ferment for 10 days. Then siphon into fermentation bottles and add the cider or Vierka "must." Fit air-lock and ferment in normal way, racking as necessary in due course. This wine, if using dried material, can be made at any time of the year. Remember to use only just sufficient elderflowers.

Elderflower and Honey

Ingredients:

2–3 pints elderflower (or a small packet of dried flowers)
Honey—mild, clover, lime, Heather, Empire—any kind will do
3 lbs.—dry recipe
6 lbs.'—sweet recipe
$\frac{1}{2}$ oz. citric acid (or 3 lemons, no pith, in lieu)
$\frac{1}{2}$ pint strong tea (or $\frac{1}{4}$ teaspoonful grape tannin)

Yeast nutrient and activated (Maury) wine yeast
Sufficient water to finally produce 1 gallon "must"

Method:

Prepare the flower heads and place them in the initial fermentation vessel and pour over the flowers the *boiling* water. Then stir in the honey until dissolved. Sugar in proportion 1 lb. to 1$\frac{1}{2}$ lb. honey may be partly or wholly substituted. If the sweet recipe is followed add the honey in several stages to avoid a "sticking" fermentation. When cool add the acid, strong tea, yeast nutrient and introduce the activated wine yeast, an extra $\frac{1}{4}$ oz. of acid and half as much again yeast nutrient may be used in this recipe if desired. Cover well and ferment for 10 days. Then siphon into fermentation bottles and fit air-lock. Leave to ferment in normal way, racking later as necessary. Never exceed 2–3 pints florets; in most cases ½ pint is sufficient, otherwise the delightful fragrance will be excessive.

Elderflower and Oak Leaf

Ingredients:

½ pint elderflowers (or a small packet of dried flowers)
½ gallon young oak leaves (or bramble tips)
4 ozs. dried bananas (or 1 pint crushed barley)
1 lb. raisins, sultanas or figs, etc.
1 level teaspoon citric acid (or 2 lemons, no pith, in lieu)
½ pint strong tea (or ¼ teaspoonful grape tannin)
3 lbs. sugar

Yeast nutrient and activated wine yeast
Sufficient water to finally produce 1 gallon "must"

Method:

Wash the oak leaves or tips, then place these in a boiler and bring to *boiling* point, cut off the heat and leave to infuse (as in tea making) for 1 hour. Place the prepared elderflowers, chopped fruits, and grains if used, together with the sugar into the initial fermentation vessel. Bring the oak leaves back to *boiling* point only and strain the extract into the initial fermentation vessel. Stir well to dissolve the sugar. When cool add the acid, strong tea, yeast nutrient, and introduce the activated wine yeast. Cover well and leave to ferment 10 days, then strain into fermentation bottles and fit air-lock, racking as necessary in due course.

Elderflower and Rhubarb

Ingredients:

½ pint elderflowers (or a small packet of dried flowers)
3 lbs. rhubarb (gooseberries or gooseberries and rhubarb may be used)
1 lb. raisins or sultanas (½ pint of white grape concentrate or
4 ozs. dried bananas may be substituted)
½ oz. citric acid (or 3 lemons, no pith, in lieu)
½ pint strong tea (or ¼ teaspoonful grape tannin)
3 lbs. sugar

Yeast nutrient and activated wine yeast
Sufficient water to finally produce 1 gallon "must"

Method:

Clean and slice the rhubarb and soak in *cold* water for 48 hours. Remember to add one Campden tablet and keep closely covered. Then prepare the elderflowers, being sure not to use any green stalks, and place these in the initial fermentation vessel together with the chopped fruits and sugar. Pour over this the *boiling* water and stir to dissolve the sugar. When cool add the rhubarb and rhubarb juice, grape concentrate if used, acid and strong tea and yeast nutrient and introduce the activated wine yeast. Closely cover and leave to ferment for 10 days. Then siphon into fermentation bottles and fit air-lock. Leave to ferment in normal way, racking as necessary in due course.

Elderflower and Rosehip

Ingredients:

$\frac{1}{2}$ pint elderflowers (or a small packet of dried flowers)
$\frac{1}{4}$ lb. dried rose hips (or 4 ozs. rosehip/shells)
1 lb. raisins, sultanas or dried apricots, etc.
$\frac{1}{2}$ oz. citric acid (or 3 lemons, no pith, in lieu)
$\frac{1}{2}$ pint strong tea (or $\frac{1}{4}$ teaspoonful grape tannin)
3 lbs. sugar
Yeast nutrient and activated wine yeast
Sufficient water to finally produce 1 gallon of "must"

Method:

Prepare the flowers and place these into the initial fermentation vessel together with the sugar and chopped fruits. Pour in the *boiling* water to dissolve the sugar and stir well. When cool add the acid, strong tea, yeast nutrient and introduce the activated wine yeast. Cover well and ferment for 10 days, then siphon into fermentation bottles and fit air lock. Leave to ferment in normal way, racking as necessary in due course. A strong, medium-sweet "social" wine with an attractive bouquet and light tawny colour.

Fig and Grape Concentrate

Ingredients:

1 lb. dried figs
1 pint grape concentrate (white or red)
4 ozs. dried bananas (or 3 ozs. dried rose hips/shells)
$2\frac{1}{2}$ lbs. sugar
$\frac{1}{4}$ oz. citric acid
$\frac{1}{4}$ pint strong tea
Yeast nutrient and activated wine yeast
Water, sufficient to finally produce 1 gallon of "must"

"Have you got a drop of vinegar I could have?"

Method:

Place the chopped fruits into the initial fermentation vessel, add the sugar, and pour in four pints of *boiling* water. Stir well with a wooden spoon to dissolve the sugar, etc. When cool (70°F.) add the citric acid, strong tea, yeast nutrient and add the grape concentrate which has been dissolved in the remainder of the warm water (*not boiling*). Be sure the "must" is not over 70°F. and introduce the activated wine yeast. Cover securely and leave to ferment 10 days, then strain into secondary fermentation vessels. Fit airlock and leave to ferment in the normal way, racking as necessary in due course.

Variation:

1. A 2 lb. tin of Australian grape jam may be used in lieu of the grape concentrate.
2. ½ lb. malt extract may be added or used in lieu of bananas.

Flower Wines

The most popular flower wines are, in order, primrose, broom, cowslip, and coltsfoot (the last being as a rule more difficult to track down). They all make delicate, light and attractive wines which are pleasant in themselves and invaluable for blending with other wines which may be lacking in bouquet.

Ingredients:

1 gallon flowers—primrose, broom, coltsfoot, cowslip (no green stalk)
1 orange, 1 lemon
3½ lbs. sugar
Yeast and nutrient

These flower wines seem to be best made as sweet wines, and 3½ lbs. sugar will give this result, but the broom wine is also agreeable when made dry, with 3 lbs. or even only 2½ lbs. of sugar to the gallon. Do not use the green stalks of the cowslip.

Method:

Bring the water to the boil and stir into it the sugar, making sure that it is all dissolved. Put the peel of the orange and lemon into a crock, bowl, or polythene bucket, being careful to exclude all white pith, to prevent the wine from having a bitter taste, and pour the hot syrup over the rinds. Allow to cool (70°F.), then add the flowers, the juice of the fruit, your chosen yeast, and some yeast nutrient. Cover closely and leave for five days in a warm place, stirring each day. Then strain through a nylon sieve into a fermenting jar, filling it to the bottom of the neck, and fit a fermentation trap. Leave for three months, then siphon the wine off the yeast deposit into a fresh jar. A further racking after another three months is helpful, and shortly after that the wine will be fit to drink, if still young.

Ginger (1)

Ingredients:

    1 oz. essence of ginger   2 lbs. granulated sugar
       (Boots)   ½ oz. tartaric acid
    ½ oz. Yeast   ½ oz. cream of tratar

Method:

Mix sugar, tartaric acid, and cream of tartar. Dissolve in four quarts of very hot water. Make up to 10 quarts adding cold/warm water so that your liquid is at about 70°F. Cream the yeast with some of the liquid and add to the bulk. Add the ginger essence and stir well. Bottle in screw stopper bottles and store at about 50–60°F. Note: Screw down stoppers tightly.

After three days, put quarter Campden tablet into each bottle. Screw down tightly again and you may drink on the fifth day. If you do not use Campden tablets you will risk bursting bottles.

The cost works out less than fourpence a bottle, is foolproof and is far superior to that you can buy.

Ginger (2)

Ingredients:

    1 oz. bruised root ginger
    ½ pint strong tea
    ¼ oz. citric acid (or 2 lemons, no pith, in lieu)
    2½ lbs. sugar
    Yeast nutrient and yeast (activated)
    Water, sufficient to produce 1 gallon of "must"

Method:

Crush the ginger and place this in the initial fermentation vessel, add the sugar and pour in the *boiling* water. Stir to dissolve the sugar. When cool (70°F.) add the citric acid, strong tea, yeast nutrient and activated yeast. Ferment for 10 days then strain into fermentation bottle. Fit air-lock and ferment in normal way, racking as necessary in due course. *The cheapest of all wines!*

Ginger (3)

(Resulting quantity about 26 pints)

Ingredients:

   $\frac{1}{2}$ gallon white concentrated grape juice of S.G. 1.385
   6 ozs. of bruised ginger
   2 ozs. of tartaric acid
   4 lbs. sugar and 1 lb. of glucose
   $\frac{1}{2}$ oz. of candied angelica (grated)

Method:

   Part "A": Mix $\frac{1}{2}$ gallon white concentrated grape juice with $1\frac{1}{2}$ gallons of water.
   Part "B": Mix 1 gallon of water with 4 lbs. of sugar; 2 ozs. tartaric acid and 6 ozs. of bruised ginger and the $\frac{1}{2}$ oz. of angelica.
   Boil ingredients of Part "B" for about 10 minutes (simmer), leave to cool, and then mix with mixture of Part "A." Add the wine culture (yeast) and leave to ferment for about 30 days when the wine should be decanted and seven days after decanted again. The wine is then ready for tasting; a rich wine.
   The 1 lb. of glucose can be added to the brew, during the fermentation process in small portions.
   The alcohol content of this wine is high.

Gooseberry (dry white)

Ingredients:

   4 lbs. gooseberries   3 lbs. sugar
   1 gallon water   Yeast and nutrient

Method:

   Wash gooseberries. Crush them in jar. Pour on one gallon *boiling* water. Cover closely and leave for 10 days. Strain off liquid and bring to boil and pour over the sugar. Stir a few seconds, leave till cool (70°F.), and add yeast and nutrient. Cover tightly again. Stir daily for seven days. Strain into fermenting jar. Fit air lock, racking as necessary in due course.

Gooseberry and Grape

Ingredients:

4 lbs. green or red gooseberries
1 pint grape concentrate (white or red)
3 lbs. sugar
2 ozs. dried bananas or 3 ozs. dried rose hips/shells
$\frac{3}{4}$ oz. glycerine (B.P. quality)
$\frac{1}{2}$ oz. citric acid (or 3 lemons, no pith, in lieu)
$\frac{1}{2}$ pint strong tea (or $\frac{1}{10}$ oz. grape tannin)
Yeast nutrient and activated wine yeast
Water; sufficient to finally produce 1 gallon "must"

Method:

Wash, then top and tail the gooseberries. Ensure that there are no flower heads or stalks left amongst the fruit, as their inclusion will give an undesirable flavour. The gooseberry does not lend itself to pressing, therefore break open the fruits and always ferment on the "pulp." Place the prepared fruit into the initial fermentation vessel, together with the dried fruit and sugar and pour in the *boiling* water, stirring well to dissolve the sugar. When cool add the citric acid, strong tea, yeast nutrient and introduce the activated wine yeast. Cover well and leave to ferment on the "pulp" seven days, then strain into fermentation bottles—avoid pressing the fruit. At this stage add the grape concentrate and glycerine. Fit air-lock and leave to ferment in the normal way, racking later as necessary.

As a variation:

$\frac{1}{4}$ pint (or $\frac{1}{2}$ packet dried) elderflowers can be introduced in the initial stage of fermentation.

Grapefruit

Ingredients:

6 sweet grapefruit
2$\frac{1}{2}$ lbs. white sugar
Yeast and nutrient

$\frac{1}{4}$ oz. pectin destroying enzyme
Water to 1 gallon

Method:

Put the thin peel from one of the fruits into a bowl, add the juice of all six and six pints of water, the yeast nutrient, the crushed Campden tablet and the pectin destroying enzyme (e.g., Pektolase or Pectozyme). Leave covered. The next day add the yeast and sugar; stir thoroughly until it is all dissolved. Leave two days, still covered, then strain into fermenting jar, make up to one gallon with cold, boiled water and fit trap. Ferment out, and rack and bottle when completely clear.

Huckleberry and Rowanberry

Ingredients:

3 lbs. huckleberries (or ¾ lb. dried bilberries)
2 lbs. rowanberries (or hawthorn berries)
1 lb. raisins (or sultanas, dates, figs, etc.)
3 lbs. sugar (or 4 lbs. honey)
½ oz. citric acid (or 3 lemons, no pith, in lieu)
½ pint strong tea (or a pinch of grape tannin)
¼ oz. pectozyme
Water to finally make up 1 gallon of "must"
Yeast nutrient and activated wine yeast

Method:

Place the berries and chopped dried fruits together with the sugar into the initial fermentation vessel (only use the garden huckleberry variety "Solanum Nigrum Var. Guinense"— other varieties may prove inedible). Pour on the *boiling* water. Macerate the fruits and stir well with a wooden spoon to break up the berries and dissolve the sugar. When cool, add the citric acid, strong tea, pectozyme and yeast nutrient. Introduce the activated wine yeast and ferment on the "pulp" for 10 days, stirring the "must" twice daily with a wooden spoon and keep closely covered. Then strain, for secondary fermentation, into fermentation vessel and fit air-lock. Leave to ferment in the normal way, racking as necessary in due course.

Lemon and Apricot

Ingredients:

½ bottle pure lemon juice (such as "P.L.J.")
1 lb. dried apricots (or figs)
3 lbs. sugar (or 4 lbs. invert sugar)
Yeast nutrient and activated wine yeast
Water; sufficient to finally produce 1 gallon of "must"

Method:

Place the chopped apricots and sugar into the initial fermentation vessel. Pour in the hot water and stir well to dissolve the sugar. When cool (70°F.) add the lemon juice and yeast nutrient. Introduce the activated wine yeast. Cover securely and leave to ferment for 10 days on the "pulp," stirring occasionally. Then strain into the secondary fermentation vessel and fit air-lock. Leave to ferment in the normal way and rack later as necessary.

Variations:

1. Add ½ lb. chopped raisins if you wish.
2. Add ¾ lb. crushed barley wheat or maize.

N.B. The lemon juice may be heavily sulphited, therefore be sure the yeast is well activated and it is desirable to add the lemon juice in stages over three days to avoid a "sticking" of the fermentation.

Lemon Thyme

This herb grows profusely in many gardens, and in late May a most pleasant wine can be made from its leaves. This recipe will produce a light and fragrant table wine not unlike a Moselle.

Ingredients:

1 pint lemon thyme leaves (no stalks)
2 lbs. raisins   1 gallon water
2½ lbs. sugar   Yeast

Method:

Chop the lemon thyme (to approximately the size of mint when making mint sauce). Pour *boiling* water over it, then add the raisins. Keep closely covered, but stir every day for 10 days. Strain on to the sugar, stir thoroughly and add yeast, wine yeast, or a level teaspoonful of granulated yeast. Leave to ferment, closely covered and in a warm place, for another two weeks. Strain into fermenting vessel and fit air lock, and leave until it has fermented right out. Ladies may prefer to add ½ lb.–1 lb. sugar to obtain a much sweeter wine but this is best added finally, to taste, and not at the outset.

Lime Juice and Raisin

Ingredients:

1 bottle pure lime juice (Rose's)
1 lb. raisins (or sultanas)
3 lbs. sugar (or 4 lbs. honey)
Yeast nutrient and activated wine yeast
Water; sufficient to finally produce 1 gallon of "must"

Method:

Place the sugar and chopped raisins into the initial fermentation vessel. Pour in the hot water and stir well to dissolve the sugar. When cool (70°F.) add the lime juice and yeast nutrient. Introduce the activated wine yeast. Cover securely and leave to ferment for 10 days on the "pulp," stirring occasionally. Then strain into the secondary fermentation vessel and fit air-lock. Leave to ferment in the normal way and rack as necessary in due course.

Variations:

1. Use a pint of grape concentrate in lieu of raisins.
2. Add 2 ozs. dried rose hips/shells if you wish or 2 ozs. dried bananas.

N.B. To avoid a "sticking" of the fermentation, be most sure to add a well activated yeast, and add the lime juice preferably in stages over three days due to the lime juice being heavily sulphited. This will disappear on refermentation.

Liqueurs

Most of the following can be made in a 2 lb. Kilner jar, or slightly larger receptacle in the case of large fruit.

ADVOCAAT

This, too, has a pleasant flavour that disguises its potency; but potent it is. Make it 9 to 10 days before serving, depending upon the weather. It "comes" more quickly in hot weather.

Ingredients:

3 eggs	6 ozs. sugar
3 juicy lemons	6 ozs. milk
Bottled pure lemon juice	6 ozs. rum

Method:

Put the eggs (raw and in their shells) into a bowl just big enough for all three to rest on the bottom. Squeeze over them juice from the lemons, adding enough bottled juice to submerge them. If the eggs float, put a cap of half a squeezed lemon on each. Cover the bowl with muslin and leave in a cool place for 8-9 days, until the egg shells dissolve, or nearly so. Then strain and squeeze (shells and all) through muslin. Beat. Add sugar. Beat. Add milk. Beat. Add rum. Beat. Bottle. Put on ice for 24 hours before serving, as a before dinner aperitif.

APRICOT BRANDY

Approximately 20 apricots
$\frac{1}{2}$ lb. of sugar
$\frac{1}{2}-\frac{3}{4}$ pint of brandy

ATHOL BROSE

This is served as a before-dinner aperitif, and should be made five days before the party. It does not keep indefinitely. And beware! It slips down so easily that your guests may not realise its potency.

Ingredients:

3 heaped dessertspoons Quaker oats (not the "instant" kind)	8 ozs. whisky
	3 dessertspoons sherry
8 ozs. cream	2 dessertspoons liquid honey

Method:

Soak the Quaker oats in water to cover. Next morning strain through muslin into a large jug. The resultant liquid is called brae. To this add cream. Stir. Add whisky. Stir. Add sherry. Stir. Add honey. Stir very thoroughly, for the honey is apt to sink to the bottom. Bottle the mixture and keep in the refrigerator until an hour or so before your guests are expected. Take it out, let it thaw a little, stir well, and pour into a bowl, ready to ladle out (stirring again) into sherry glasses.

BLACKBERRY BRANDY (See Cassis)

CASSIS (same proportions for blackberry liqueur)
$\frac{3}{4}$ fill jar with crushed blackcurrants
6 ozs. sugar per pint capacity
Top up with gin or other spirit

CHERRY BRANDY
1 lb. morello cherries
$\frac{1}{2}$ lb. castor sugar
12 almonds
Top up with brandy

CREME DE MENTHE

Sounds expensive when you learn that the base is two bottles of gin. But when you realise that this makes nearly three bottles of liqueur, of which far less is consumed per person than when gin is drunk in the usual ways, and, moreover, that you only drink it on occasion, and that it keeps indefinitely, you may revise your opinion.

Note. Before producing it at the dinner table, make sure to loosen the cork or stopper of bottle or decanter. The sugar content is apt to make it stick.

Required:

3 empty gin (or other) bottles	2 bottles gin
2 lbs. 4 ozs. granulated sugar	Peppermint essence
	Green colouring

DAMSON GIN
1 lb. damsons
6 ozs. sugar
Top up with gin

Into each bottle pour 12 ozs. sugar, then fill with gin to within 1 inch of neck. Cork. Several times a day (i.e., whenever you pass the bottles) shake, and in four or five days, when the liquid is quite clear, add (to taste) about two teaspoons peppermint essence and about the same of green colouring. Shake once or twice to spread flavour and colour, then cork again and set aside. Mark the date on the bottle and try to give it three months to mature.

DAMSON GIN

And this damson gin recipe is highly recommended by Mr. William A. Walker, of 601 South Red Bank Road, Evansville, Indiana 47712.

Ingredients:

3 lbs. damsons	1 quart dry gin
3 lbs. sugar	

Method:

Puncture each damson five or six times with a fork and drop into a wide mouth gallon jug. Add 3 lbs. sugar and 1 quart gin. Lay the jug on its side as far as possible and each day rotate half turn. Do not shake. When most of the sugar has dissolved the damson gin is ready for use. Believe you me, this is a drink fit for Jupiter! Use sparingly.

FRAMBOISE

1 lb. raspberries
¾ lb. castor sugar
Spirit

MULBERRY LIQUEUR

1 pint of sound mulberries
4–6 ozs. castor sugar
Top up with brandy or gin

PEACH BRANDY

Half fill jar with halved peaches
¼ lb. castor sugar
¼ lb. brown sugar
A few kernels from the peach stones. Top up with brandy.

PRUNELLE

¾ jar of ripe sound plums
6 ozs. castor sugar
A few kernels from the plum stones. Top up with spirit.

RED-CURRANT LIQUEUR (see blackcurrant liqueur or cassis)

SLOE GIN (October or November)

1 lb. sloes
3–4 ozs. castor sugar
Top up with gin
½ dozen blanched almonds or a small eggspoon of almond essence.

WHITE-CURRANT LIQUEUR

1 teaspoon of grated lemon rind
1½ lbs. white-currants
1 lb. castor sugar
A few small pieces of lemon rind
A small teaspoon of ginger essence
Top up the jar with whisky

A MINT FAVOURITE

Strip the leaves off a couple of good sprigs of mint and crush them. Put the crushed leaves into a jug and add three tablespoons of castor sugar. Pour in just enough hot water to dissolve the sugar, add a wineglass of liqueur brandy and fill up with iced water.

ANOTHER MINT FAVOURITE

Thoroughly bruise a few sprigs of mint and place in a lager-type glass. Add two or three tablespoons of crushed ice, and fill up with equal quantities of chilled wine and soda water. Most peope like this dry, but sweet-tooths will want to add a little sugar.

Loganberry and Beetroot

Ingredients:

3 lbs. loganberries (or blackberries)

2 lbs. beetroot

1 pint commercial or home-made cider (or $\frac{1}{4}$ bottle Vierka concentrated must)

3 lbs. sugar

2 lemons

$\frac{1}{4}$ oz. Pectinol

Water to finally make up 1 gallon of "must"

Yeast nutrient and activated wine yeast

Method:

Wash the beetroot, (do not peel) and slice into thin rings. Place in a saucepan and simmer in the usual way until tender. Place the berries and sugar into the initial fermentation vessel and strain into this the hot beetroot liquor. Macerate and stir well with a wooden spoon to break up the berries and to dissolve the sugar. When *cool* add the cider or concentrated "must," lemon juice, pectinol and yeast nutrient. Introduce the activated wine yeast and ferment on the "pulp" for 10 days, stirring the must twice

daily with a wooden spoon, and keep it closely covered. Then strain, for secondary fermentation, into fermentation vessel and fit air-lock. Leave to ferment in the normal way, racking as necessary in due course.

Loganberry and Blackcurrant

Ingredients:

> 4 lbs. loganberries
> 2 lbs. blackcurrants (or 1 lb. red-currants)
> ¼ oz. citric acid (or 2 lemons, no pith)
> 1/16 oz. grape tannin (or ½ pint strong tea)
> 3 lbs. sugar
> Yeast nutrient and activated wine yeast
> Water; sufficient to finally produce 1 gallon of "must"

Method:

Place the fruits into the initial fermentation vessel and macerate these with a wooden spoon, then pour in the *boiling* water, add the sugar and stir well until dissolved. When cool add the acid, tannin (and ½ oz. pectozyme if you wish), yeast nutrient and introduce the activated wine yeast and secure closely, leaving to ferment for five days. Then transfer through nylon strainer into fermentation bottles. Fit air-lock and leave to ferment in normal way, racking, as necessary in due course. A Burgundy yeast is recommended.

Variations:

1. ½ lb. malt extract may be added.
2. ¾ oz. glycerine may be added at the final fermentation stage, i.e., when fitting the air-lock.

Loganberry and Crab Apple

Ingredients:

> 3 lbs. (or more) loganberries (or blackberries)
> 4 lbs. crab apples) or mixed apples)
> 1 lb. raisins (dried figs, dates, prunes or apricots, etc., may be substituted)
> 3 lbs. sugar
> ½ pint strong tea (or pinch of grape tannin)
> ½ oz. citric acid (or 3 lemons, no pith, in lieu)
> ½ oz. pektolase
> Water to finally make up to 1 gallon of "must"
> Yeast nutrient and activated wine yeast

Method:

Wash and cut up the apples into small pieces, skins included, and place these together with the berries, chopped dried fruits and sugar into initial fermentation vessel. Pour in the *boiling* water, macerate and stir well with a wooden spoon to break up the berries and to dissolve the sugar. When cool add the strong tea, citric acid, pektolase and yeast nutrient. Introduce the activated wine yeast and ferment on the "pulp" for 10 days, stirring the "must" twice daily with a wooden spoon and keep it closely covered. Then strain, for secondary fermentation, in fermentation vessel and fit air-lock. Leave to ferment in the normal way, racking as necessary in due course.

Loganberry and Plum

Ingredients:

3 lbs. loganberries (or blackberries)
2 lbs. plums (or greengages)
4 ozs. dried bananas (or 2 lbs. fresh bananas, including skins)
3 lbs. sugar
2 lemons
½ oz. pektolase
Water to make up finally 1 gallon of "must"
Yeast nutrient and activated wine yeast

Method:

Place the loganberries into the initial fermentation vessel and add the stoned plums, sugar and either dried bananas or chopped fresh bananas including skins, then pour on to these the *boiling* water. Mash the fruits with a wooden spoon and stir well to dissolve the sugar. When cool add the lemon juice, pektolase and yeast nutrient. Introduce the activated wine yeast and ferment on the "pulp" for 10 days, stirring the "must" twice daily with a wooden spoon and keeping it closely covered, then strain, for secondary fermentation, into fermentation vessel and fit air-lock. Leave to ferment in the normal way, racking as necessary in due course.

Lovage

Ingredients:

1 gallon lovage, florets only
1 lb. malt extract (or 1 lb. raisins, etc.)
3 lbs. sugar
½ pint strong tea (or a pinch of grape tannin)
½ oz. citric acid (or 3 lemons, no pith, in lieu)
Water to finally make up 1 gallon of "must"
Yeast and activated wine yeast

Method:

Place the florets, malt extract (or chopped fruit) and sugar into the initial fermentation vessel. Pour in the *boiling* water and stir with a wooden spoon to dissolve the sugar and malt extract. When cool add the strong tea, citric acid, and yeast nutrient. Introduce the activated wine yeast and ferment on the "pulp" for 10 days, stirring the "must" twice daily with a wooden spoon and keep it closely covered. Then strain for secondary fermentation, into fermentation vessel and fit air-lock. Leave to ferment in the normal way, racking as necessary in due course.

Lovage and Nettle

Ingredients:

    1 lb. lovage leaves (Levisticum Officinale)
    1 lb. nettles
    2 lbs. bananas including skins (or 4 ozs. dried bananas)
    1 lb. figs (or dates, sultanas, prunes, etc.)
    3 lbs. sugar
    ½ pint strong tea (or a pinch of grape tannin)
    ½ oz. citric acid (or 3 lemons, no pith, in lieu)
    Water to finally make up 1 gallon "must"
    Yeast nutrient and activated wine yeast

Method:

Shred the lovage leaves and nettles. Place these together with the chopped fruits and sugar into the initial fermentation vessel. Pour in the *boiling* water. Macerate and stir well with a wooden spoon to break up the fruit and to dissolve the sugar. When cool add the citric acid, strong tea and yeast nutrient. Introduce the activated wine yeast and ferment on the "pulp" for 10 days, stirring the "must" twice daily with a wooden spoon and keep it closely covered. Then strain, for secondary fermentation, into fermentation vessel and fit air-lock. Leave to ferment in the normal way, racking as necessary.

Maize

Ingredients:

    1 pint maize   2 lemons
    Soak the maize overnight   1 orange
    2 lbs. raisins   4 lbs. Demerara sugar
    1 gallon water
    Yeast and yeast nutrient

Method:

Crush the maize in a mincer and put it into a crock with the chopped raisins, thinly peeled lemon rinds, fruit juice, sugar and yeast nutrient. Pour on the *boiling* water, stir to dissolve sugar, and leave till cool; then add yeast. Keep well covered in a warm place for three weeks, stirring daily, then strain into fermenting bottle and fit trap. Leave to ferment right out and clear, then bottle.

Mangold

Ingredients:

5 lbs. mangolds
1 gallon water
3 lbs. sugar
  (for a medium wine) or
2½ lbs. sugar
  (for a dry table wine)

2 lemons
2 oranges
Yeast and nutrient

Method:

Wash the mangolds but do not peel. Cut into pieces and boil until tender. Strain, and to each gallon of liquor add the sugar and the rinds of the oranges and lemons (avoiding the white pith). Boil for 20 minutes. Allow the liquor to cool, and add the juice of the oranges and lemons. Stir in the yeast and leave in a warm place, well covered, for about a week. Then stir before transferring jar, and fit air-lock. Leave in a temperature of about 65°F. until it clears, then rack into clean jar and refit lock. Bottle after a further two months.

Mangold and Caraway

Ingredients:

5 lbs. mangolds
1 lb. chopped raisins (or sultanas, dates, etc.)
2½ lbs. sugar (or 3 lbs. honey)
½ oz. citric acid (or 3 lemons, no pith)
1 oz. caraway seeds
1 tablespoon strong tea
Water to make up finally 1 gallon of "must"
Yeast nutrient and activated wine yeast

Method:

Scrub and cut up the beet. Simmer in seven pints water for 1½ hours, together with the caraway seeds. Pour the beet, seeds and liquor into the initial fermentation vessel in which the chopped fruits and sugar have already been placed. Stir well with a wooden spoon to dissolve the sugar, etc. When cool add the strong tea, citric acid and yeast nutrient. Introduce the activated wine yeast and ferment on the "pulp" for 10 days, stirring the "must" with a wooden spoon, twice daily, and ensuring that it is closely covered. Then strain, for secondary fermentation, into fermentation vessel and fit air-lock. Leave to ferment in the normal way, racking as necessary in due course.

Marigold

Marigolds (Calendula) are grown in nearly every garden from seed, their lovely orange colour adds much gaiety to the garden. Their medicinal properties are well known and wine made from the flower heads possesses many virtues.

Old-time Recipe:

One peck of marigold petals, 1½ lbs. stoned raisins, 7 lbs. castor sugar, 2 lbs. honey, 3 gallons water, 3 eggs, 6 oranges, 4 tablespoonsful German yeast, 1 oz. gelatine, 1 lb. sugar candy, 1 pint brandy.

Method:

Take a peck of marigold flowers, and put them into an earthenware bowl with the raisins. Pour over them a *boiling* liquid made of the sugar, honey, and 3 gallons of water. Clear this liquid while it is *boiling* with the whites and shells of three eggs and strain it before putting it in the flowers. Cover up the bowl and leave it for two days and nights. Stir it well and leave it for another day and night. Then strain it and put it into a six gallon cask which has been well cleansed, and add to it 1 lb. sugar candy and the rinds of six oranges, which have been peeled and stripped of all white pith. Stir into it four tablespoonsful of German yeast and cover up the bung hole. Leave it to work till it froths out. When the fermentation is over pour in a pint of brandy and ½ oz. dissolved gelatine. Stop the cask and leave it for several months before bottling.

Modern Basic Recipe:

2 quarts marigold heads	1oz. citric acid
4 lbs. sugar	Yeast nutrient
1 lb. raisins (chopped)	Yeast culture
1 gallon water	1 cup cold tea

Method:

The marigolds should be gathered at the full strength of the midday sun when they are wide open and only the golden petals should be used. Dissolve the sugar in the water, add the chopped raisins and allow to cool. Add the crushed flower heads, citric acid (or lemons and oranges—no pith) and cold tea. When at right temperature add yeast nutrient and yeast culture. Leave for five days, stirring twice daily.

Marrow and Prune

Ingredients:

5 lbs. ripe marrow
1 lb. prunes (dates, peaches, sultanas, figs, etc., may be used
  in lieu)
2 ozs. dried rose/hips/shells
3 lbs. sugar
2 lemons
Water to finally make up 1 gallon of "must"
Yeast nutrient and activated wine yeast

Method:

Shred the marrow and chop the prunes and place these together with the marrow seeds, sugar and rose hips/shells into the initial fermentation vessel. Pour in the *boiling* water and stir well with a wooden spoon to dissolve the sugar. When cool add the juice of the lemons and yeast nutrient. Introduce the activated wine yeast and ferment on the "pulp" for 10 days, stirring the must twice daily with a wooden spoon and keep it closely covered. Then strain, for secondary fermentation, into a fermentation vessel and fit air-lock. Leave to ferment in the normal way, racking as necessary in due course.

May (Hawthorn Blossom)

Ingredients:

2 quarts hawthorn flowers	1 gallon water
3½ lbs. white sugar	2 lemons
Yeast	Yeast nutrient

Method:

Boil up the sugar and lemon rind (no white pith) in water for 30 minutes, adding more water if necessary to retain the volume. Pour into a bowl and when cool add the yeast, the lemon juice, and the yeast nutrient. Leave for eight days, stirring daily, then strain through muslin into fermenting bottle and fit trap. Leave until it clears, then siphon off and bottle.

Meads

MEAD
Ingredients:

4 lbs. English honey	Yeast
1 gallon water	Yeast nutrient
1 lemon, 1 orange	

Method:

Bring the honey in the water to the boil, and leave to cool in a bowl. Add the juice of the citrus fruit, the yeast nutrient, and the yeast, pour into a fermenting bottle and fit air-lock. Mead sometimes takes rather long to ferment but when it is clear and fermentation has ceased siphon off into clean bottles and leave to mature.

MELOMEL (A fruit-flavoured mead)

Ingredients:

3½ lbs. honey	Juice of 2 lemons
½ lb. dried rose hips	Yeast and nutrient
1 gallon water	

Method:

Soak the dried rosehips in a little of the water for 24 hours. Then return them (and their water) to the rest of the gallon, bring to the boil, and simmer for 10 minutes. Add the honey and stir until dissolved. Strain into a fermenting jar when cool, and add the juice of the two lemons and the yeast nutrient. When the temperature has dropped to 21°C. (70°F.) add the yeast, preferably a Maury yeast. Ferment and rack as usual. Mead fermentations, it should be noted, are often rather lengthy.

MELOMEL APERITIF

Ingredients:

4 pints orange juice	Nutrients
Peel from 12 oranges	Madeira yeast starter
1 pint white grape concentrate	Water to 1 gallon
1½ lbs. clover honey	

Method:

Express the juice from sufficient oranges to give four pints orange juice. Add the grape concentrate, dissolve the honey in this blend and make the volume up to one gallon with water. Add the nutrients and 100 ppm. sulphite (2 Campden tablets). After 24 hours, introduce the yeast and the peel from 12 oranges (no pith should be included). Ferment to dryness and thereafter proceed as directed in the basic procedure, removing the orange peel at the first racking. Fortification may be practised if desired.

TABLE MELOMEL

Ingredients:

6 pints pear juice	Nutrients
1 pint white grape concentrate	Champagne yeast starter
1 lb. acacia blossom honey	Water to 1 gallon
$\frac{1}{2}$ pint yellow rose petals	

Method:

Express the juice from sufficient pears (12–14 lbs.) to give six pints juice. Dissolve the honey and nutrients in this juice and add 100 ppm. sulphite (2 Campden tablets). After 24 hours add the yeast starter. Allow to ferment for seven days, then add the rose petals. After a further three days, strain off the rose petals and make the volume up to one gallon with water. Ferment to dryness and thereafter proceed as instructed in the basic procedure.

Note: An excellent sparkling wine can be made from this recipe by reducing the amount of honey to $\frac{3}{4}$ lb. and using honey instead of sugar to prime the bottles prior to the bottle fermentation. Careful control is necessary to be successful here, but outstanding sparkling wines can be obtained in this manner, especially if perry pears are available. For full details of sparkling wine production—see the companion book in this series—"Making Wines Like Those You Buy."

PIPPIN CYSER

Ingredients:

8 pints Cox's Orange Pippin juice	Nutrients
2 lbs. acacia blossom honey	Sauternes yeast starter

Method:

Express the juice from sufficient Cox's Orange Pippins to give eight pints of juice (about 16 lbs. apples required). Dissolve the honey in this juice, add 100 ppm. sulphite (2 Campden tablets) and leave to settle for 24 hours. Rack off the juice from the sediment which has been deposited, then add the nutrients and yeast starter. Ferment until the gravity drops to 12 and rack. Rack again as soon as fermentation restarts and add 50 ppm. sulphite (1 Campden tablet). Thereafter proceed as directed in the basic procedure.

Note: This wine will mature well and 10-gallon quantities will benefit from spending 6–12 months in cask prior to bottling. Most winemakers will be unable to make this quantity, of course, but those who can will never regret doing so!

ROSE CYSER

Ingredients:

4 pints apple juice   1 lb. clover honey
1 pint white grape concentrate   Nutrients
½ pint yellow rose petals   Steinberg yeast starter

Method:

Express the juice from sufficient apples (8–10 lbs.) to give four pints juice. Add two pints water and dissolve the honey and nutrients in the diluted apple juice. Add 100 ppm. sulphite (2 Campden tablets) and leave to settle for 24 hours. Blend in the grape concentrate and introduce the yeast. After seven days add the rose petals and strain off three days later. Make the volume up to 1 gallon with water, ferment to dryness and thereafter continue as directed in the basic procedure.

Note: An interesting variation which gives a rosé wine can be tried by substituting part of the grape concentrate and/or red rose petals by red grape concentrate and red rose petals. Canned apple juice can also be used in place of fresh apple juice if desired.

Morello Cherry

Ingredients:

8 lbs. cracked and windfall   3½ lbs. preserving sugar
     Morello cherries   Yeast
1 gallon water

Method:

Stalk and wash the fruit, place in a crock, and add one pint of cold water to each pound of fruit, and then one crushed Campden tablet (per gallon). Lastly add a level teaspoonful of dried yeast. Leave for 10 days, keeping closely covered, but stir well each day and mash the fruit with the hands. Strain mixture through nylon sieve into gallon jar, add the sugar, and top up with water. Agitate well to dissolve sugar. When vigorous fermentation dies down, fit air-lock. Ferment out, rack, and bottle in usual way.

Mulberry

Ingredients:

9 lbs. mulberries (this wine needs a heavy fruit content)
1 lb. raisins
3 lbs. sugar
2 lemons
¼ oz. Pectolase
Water to finally make up 1 gallon of "must"
Yeast nutrient and activated wine yeast

72

Method:

Place the mulberries, chopped raisins and sugar into the initial fermentation vessel, and crush the mulberries by stirring with a wooden spoon. Then pour in the *boiling* water and stir to dissolve the sugar. When cool (70°F.) add the lemon juice, pektolase and yeast nutrient. Introduce the activated wine yeast (Burgundy or Port wine yeasts are suggested) and ferment on the "pulp" for 10 days, stirring each day with a wooden spoon and ensuring that the "must" is closely covered. Then strain into the secondary fermentation vessel and leave to ferment under the protection of a fermentation lock, racking as necessary in due course.

Mulls

"How you totter, good feet! Have a care of my bones! If you fail me, I pass all the night on these stones."

—William Terrington.

MULLED ALE (To make 9 wine glasses)

Ingredients:

2 pints ale (brown ale is best)	1 pinch each of ground
1 tablespoon castor sugar	cloves, nutmeg, ginger
	1 wineglass rum or brandy

Method:

Put ale, sugar and spices in saucepan and bring nearly to boiling point. Add brandy or rum and serve at once while still very hot.

MULLED CIDER

Ingredients:

1 gallon cider	1½ teaspoonsful of allspice
1½ cups brown sugar	1½ sticks of cinnamon
½ teaspoonful ginger	½ teaspoonful nutmeg
1½ teaspoonsful of cloves	½ teaspoonful salt

Method:

Place the sugar, spices, cider and salt into the saucepan, heat and simmer for 20 minutes, strain through muslin or fine nylon strainer and rinse out saucepan. Then return the strained liquor to the saucepan and reheat until piping hot (avoid boiling). Serves 15 beakers or mugs according to size. Hot mulled cider is an excellent "goodnight friends" drink on a chilly night.

MULLED CIDER

Ingredients:

> 1 quart cider   Sugar to taste
> 3 eggs

Method:

Add the sugar to the cider to adjust acidity to taste and bring to almost boiling point. Pour the heated liquor over the whisked eggs and stir well. Return the mixture to the saucepan and reheat and serve in glasses piping hot.

MULLED ELDERBERRY

Ingredients:

> 1 bottle medium sweet 1" stick of cinnamon
> elderberry wine   ½ teaspoon allspice
> 2 ozs. loaf sugar   Orange and lemon rind
> 3 or 4 cloves   Angostura bitters

Method:

Pour the wine into a sound enamel saucepan, add sugar, cloves, spices and a few curls of orange and lemon rind. Heat without boiling and strain into a warm jug. Add half teaspoon Angostura bitters and a little hot water to taste. Serve with a pinch or nutmeg in earthenware mugs.

MULLED STOUT (and ale too!)
Method:

Pour the stout or ale into a pewter tankard and immerse a red hot poker. Take precautions to avoid overflowing!

VINTNERS' MULL
Ingredients:

> 1 bottle sweet wine   Ground ginger
> 1 wine glass apricot brandy Castor sugar
> 1 large sweet orange   ½ pint boiling water

Method:

Stud the orange with the cloves and bake for one hour. Heat the wine, brandy and ginger to almost boiling point—remember *boiling* drives off the alcohol and robs the brew of its potency—with the baked orange floating on top and add the sugar to suit one's own taste—a further ½ pint of *boiling* water may be added just before serving—if you are feeling economical.

"I'm making mead"

WASSAIL BOWL

*"In the Wassail Bowl we'll drink unto thee Wassail! Wassail!
Wassail!"*

Ingredients:

1 quart beer or ale	A few slices of lemon rind
¼ teaspoonful ginger	(no pith)
¼ teaspoonful nutmeg	½ pint sherry
¼ teaspoonful ground	Sugar to taste
cinnamon	6 crab apples or 3 rosy red
	apples

Method:

Heat the sherry and ale together with the spices and lemon rind and simmer for five minutes. Prior to this bake the apples until they are just soft and baste well whilst cooking with ale and sugar. Then add these to the spiced liquor adding extra sugar to taste. Serve really piping hot in tankards.

The foregoing is just a few examples of how you can vary the method of serving your home-made wines, ciders and beers, but remember if you are drinking alcohol in quantity you will need something to eat!

Meadowsweet

(Filipendula Ulmaria)

"The floures boiled in wine and drunke, do make the heart merrie"
—Gerrard.

Ingredients:

1 gallon meadowsweet flowers (heads only) (or 1 packet dried heads)
1 lb. raisins (dried figs, dates, prunes, or apricots, etc., may be substituted)
3 lbs. sugar
½ pint strong tea (or a pinch of grape tannin)
½ oz. Citric acid (or 3 lemons, no pith, in lieu)
Water to finally make up 1 gallon "must"
Yeast nutrient and activated wine yeast

Method:

Place the flowers, chopped fruit, and sugar into the initial fermentation vessel. Pour in the *boiling* water and stir well with a wooden spoon to dissolve the sugar, etc. When cool add the citric acid, strong tea and yeast nutrient. Introduce the activated wine yeast and ferment on the "pulp" for 10 days, stirring the "must" twice daily with a wooden spoon and keep it closely covered. Then strain for secondary fermentation, in a fermentation vessel and fit air-lock. Leave to ferment in the normal way, racking as necessary in due course.

Meadowsweet and Banana

Ingredients:

1 packet of dried meadowsweet herb (Filipendula Ulmaria)
(1 lb. fresh herb or 2 ozs. dried herb)
4 ozs. dried bananas (or 2 lbs. fresh bananas with skins)
1 lb. raisins or sultanas
3 lbs. sugar (or 3½ lbs. honey)
¼ oz. citric acid (or 2 lemons, no pith, in lieu)
1/16 oz. grape tannin (or 1 tablespoon strong tea)
Water to make up finally 1 gallon of "must"
Yeast nutrient and activated wine yeast

Method:

Place the herb, chopped fruits and sugar into the initial fermentation vessel. Pour in the *boiling* water and stir with a wooden spoon to dissolve the sugar, etc. When cool add the citric acid, grape tannin and yeast nutrient. Introduce the activated wine yeast and ferment on the "pulp" for 10 days, stirring the "must" with a wooden spoon, twice daily, ensuring that the "must" is closely covered. Then strain, for secondary fermentation, into fermentation vessel, and fit air-lock. Leave to ferment in the normal way, racking as necessary in due course.

Medlar and Rosehip

Ingredients:

3 lbs. medlars (picked November and stored 3 weeks or so until almost overripe)
8 ozs. dried rose hips or 4 ozs. shells
2 ozs. dried bananas (or 1 lb. bananas including skins)
3 lbs. sugar (or 4 lbs. honey)
½ oz. citric acid (or 3 lemons, no pith, in lieu)
½ pint strong tea (or a pinch of grape tannin)
½ oz. Pektolase
Water to finally make up 1 gallon of "must"
Yeast nutrient and activated wine yeast

Method:

It is essential to store the medlars until it is almost overripe otherwise the slightly acid taste is not brought out until it has been stored for three weeks or more.

Place the fruits, together with the sugar, into the initial fermentation vessel. Pour in the *boiling* water. Macerate and stir well with a wooden spoon to break up the fruit and to dissolve the sugar. When cool, add the citric acid, strong tea, pektolase and yeast nutrients. Introduce the activated wine yeast and ferment on the "pulp" for 10 days stirring the "must" twice daily with a wooden spoon and keep it closely covered. Then strain, for secondary fermentation, into fermentation vessel, and fit air-lock. Leave to ferment in the normal way, racking as necessary in due course.

Mint

Ingredients:

> 1½ pints mint leaves (lightly bruised)
> ½ pint strong tea
> 3½ lbs. sugar
> 2 lemons or ¼ oz. citric acid
> Yeast nutrient
> Yeast
> 1 gallon water

Method:

Pour *boiling* water over the sugar and mint leaves. Stir well. Infuse for 24 hours, then add the lemon juice, yeast and nutrient. Forty-eight hours later strain into one gallon jar and make up to one gallon if necessary. Ferment, rack and bottle as usual.

Mint Suprise

Ingredients:

> 4–6 ozs. well-bruised mint leaves, including chopped stalks
> (1½ ozs. dried mint may be used in lieu)
> 3 lbs. rhubarb
> 9 pints water
> 1 lb. barley or wheat (crushed)
> ½ pint strong tea
> 4 lbs. sugar
> Yeast nutrient and selected wine yeast

Method:

Soak the grain in one pint of water overnight, then run through a mincer. Add the crushed rhubarb. Boil the mint in eight pints of water for 15 minutes, then pour over the grain and rhubarb, add sugar, stir well. When cool add the strong tea. Then Add the yeast nutrient and activated wine yeast. Ferment on solids 7–10 days, then strain into fermentation vessel and allow to finish in normal way.

Minteano

Recipe by the late Mr. F. G. Spark, of 88 Old Winton Road, Andover, who specialised in spiced and unusual wines:

"Save tea left over from the tea pot until you have nearly 1½ pints, then add 6 ozs. sugar and 2 ozs. chopped raisins or sultanas and a saltspoon of Heath and Heather dried yeast, and cork lightly or plug with cotton wool. This will start to ferment and thus save mould growing on the surface of the "must" while you are collecting another quart or more in other bottles until you have one gallon, using the same amount of sugar and raisins for each quart. When you have your gallon add a handful of chopped mint and the juice of two lemons or one level teaspoonful of citric acid, fit air-lock and ferment for one month, then strain, and proceed in the usual manner until fermentation ceases. Keep for one year and you will have a very fine and unusual wine."

Mixed Soft Fruit

Ingredients:

> 5 lbs. any soft fruit—mixed or otherwise (1¼ lbs. dried bilberries may be used instead)
> 4 pints cider
> 1 oz. root ginger
> 1 teaspoonful each dried Rosemary and Lavender leaves (optional)
> 1¼ ozs. cream of tartar
> 3 lbs. sugar (or 4 lbs. honey)
> $\frac{1}{16}$ oz. grape tannin (or ½ pint strong tea)
> Yeast nutrient and activated wine yeast
> Water: sufficient to prodice 1 gallon of "must"

Method:

Prepare the fruits ensuring that there are no leaves or stalks used. Macerate with a wooden spoon, then add the root ginger, herbs, if used, and sugar and place these in the initial fermentation vessel. Pour in two pints of *boiling* water and stir well to dissolve the sugar. When cool add the cream of tartar, tannin, yeast nutrient, cider and activated wine yeast. Cover well and ferment five days, then strain through a nylon sieve into glass fermentation bottles. Fit air-lock and leave to ferment in normal way, racking as necessary in due course. The use of mixed fruits gives a better "balance" than using a single fruit.

Variations:

½ lb. of malt extract may be used as an additive to give "body."

Nectarine

Ingredients:

> 3½ lbs. nectarines (or peaches in lieu)
> 2 ozs. dried bananas
> 3 lbs. sugar
> ½ oz. citric acid (or 3 lemons, no pith, in lieu)
> ½ pint strong tea (or a pinch of grape tannin)
> ¼ oz. pectozyme
> Water to finally make up 1 gallon of "must"
> Yeast nutrient and activated wine yeast

Method:

Clean and stone the nectarines and place these together with the dried bananas and sugar into the initial fermentation vessel. Pour in the *boiling* water, macerate and stir well with a wooden spoon to break up the fruit and to dissolve the sugar. When cool add the citric acid, strong tea, pectozyme and yeast nutrient. Introduce the activated wine yeast and ferment on the "pulp" for 10 days, stirring the "must" twice daily with a wooden spoon and keep it closely covered. Then strain, for secondary fermentation, into fermentation vessel and fit air-lock. Leave to ferment in the normal way, racking as necessary in due course.

Oak Leaf

Ingredients:

60 young oak leaves	Yeast nutrient
3 lbs. sugar	Selected wine yeast
3 lemons	1 gallon water
3 oranges or $\frac{1}{2}$ oz. citric acid	

Method:

Cleanse the leaves by swirling them in cold water and drain off. Pour the one gallon of *boiling* water over the leaves and allow them to infuse for 24 hours. Strain, then simmer the liquid to obtain sufficient heat to enable liquid to dissolve the sugar. Pour the hot extract over the sugar, add the lemon and orange juices or citric acid, and stir well. The grated peel of the oranges (no pith) should be simmered in a little of the liquid for 15 minutes and the resulting liquid is then returned to the bulk. When cool make up to the gallon again with water, if necessary, add the yeast nutrient, introduce an activated general purpose wine yeast and allow fermentation to proceed (using air-locks) in the normal way. Fully matured leaves or leaves in early autumn that are changing colour may be used to give variations, as may walnut leaves.

Onion

Ingredients:

$\frac{1}{2}$ lb. onions	2 lemons or citric acid
$\frac{1}{2}$ lb. potatoes	Yeast nutrient
1 lb. chopped raisins	Yeast (selected wine)
3 lbs. sugar	

Method:

Slice and dice the onions and potatoes and place these together with the chopped raisins in warm (not hot) water in which the sugar has been dissolved. Add lemon juice (no pith) or citric acid and yeast nutrient, then introduce activated yeast. Ferment for 10 days, then strain and complete fermentation in glass jars under fermentation lock.

Orange Peel (dried)

Ingredients:

1 pint of pieces of dried peel   2½ lbs. sugar
¼ oz. root ginger   1 gallon of boiling water
½ lb. raisins or sultanas

Method:

Pour the *boiling* water over the peel and leave for three days. Remove the peel and add ginger, raisins and sugar, and ferment with wine yeast. When fermentation quietens, after about a week, strain into fermenting jar and fit trap. The 2½ lbs. sugar gives a dry wine and this quantity can be increased if required.

Seville Orange

Ingredients:

12 thin skinned Seville oranges   3½ lbs. white sugar
2 lemons   1 gallon water

Method:

Peel six of the oranges and throw away the peel. Cut up oranges and lemons into slices and put into earthenware pan. Boil the water and pour on boiling. Place in moderately warm corner and when tepid add yeast, a good wine yeast or a level teaspoonful of granulated yeast; stir each day for a fortnight. Strain all through a sieve, then add sugar and stir until dissolved. Put in 1-gallon jar, filling up to top. Put surplus in dark bottles (bottles must be coloured or wine will lose its colour). Use this for filling up large jar. Ferment to completion under air-lock, rack when it clears, and bottle two months later.

Orange and Banana

Ingredients:

8 oranges
1 lb. bananas (or 2 ozs. dried variety)
$\frac{1}{2}$ lb. raisins or (sultanas)
$\frac{1}{4}$ pint strong tea
3 lbs. sugar
Yeast nutrient and activated wine yeast
Water: sufficient to finally produce 1 gallon of "must"

Method:

Peel the oranges very thinly, avoiding the white pith which imparts a very undesirable bitterness. Cut the oranges in half and squeeze out the juice. Place the juice and remainder of the fruit, minus the pith, together with the chopped bananas and raisins into the initial fermentation vessel. Add the sugar and pour in three-quarters of the water, almost boiling hot, and stir with a wooden spoon to dissolve the sugar. The remaining quart of water should be placed in a saucepan together with the orange peel and this be allowed to simmer for 30 minutes. When cool (70°F.) add the strong tea and yeast nutrient. Introduce the activated wine yeast, cover securely and leave to ferment for 10 days on the pulp, stirring occasionally, then strain into secondary fermentation vessel. Fit air-lock and leave to ferment in the normal way, racking in due course as necessary.

Orange and Raisin

Ingredients:

3 Jaffa oranges
3 Seville oranges
6 sweet oranges
2 lemons

1 lb. raisins
3 lbs. sugar
1 gallon water
Yeast nutrient and activated wine yeast

Method:

Peel the oranges and lemons very thinly and discard the pith. Put the skins into the oven, and bake them until they are browned then pour over them a quart of *boiling* water and infuse as for making tea. Place the sugar into the initial fermentation vessel, add boiling water to dissolve sugar. When cool add the chopped raisins, pulped oranges and lemons, and the infusion from the skins. Add the yeast nutrient and activated wine yeast. Ferment on the "pulp" for 10 days then strain into fermentation bottles. Fit air-lock and leave to ferment in the normal way, racking as necessary in due course.

Parsley

Ingredients:

1 lb. fresh parsley	Lump of ginger
3 lbs. sugar	2 lemons
5 quarts water	Yeast

Method:

Well wash and boil parsley until tender, strain into an earthenware crock. Add sugar, ginger and sliced lemons. Stir well until the sugar is dissolved. When cooled to blood heat add yeast and leave closely covered for a fortnight, stirring daily. Then strain into fermenting jar and fit trap. Siphon off when wine has cleared and keep for at least a further six months.

Parsley and Apricot

Ingredients:

1 lb. fresh parsley, including stalks (or 1 packet of dried parsley)

1 lb. dried apricots (or 3 lbs. fresh apricots)

2 ozs. dried bananas (or dried rose hips/shells)

3 lbs. sugar

$\frac{1}{2}$ pint strong tea (or a pinch of grape tannin)

2 lemons

$\frac{1}{4}$ oz. Pectolase

Water to finally make up 1 gallon of "must"

Yeast nutrient and activated wine yeast

Method:

Cut up the parsley and simmer for 20 minutes. Place the chopped fruits and sugar into the initial fermentation vessel, then pour in the parsley and parsley liquor. Stir well with a wooden spoon to dissolve the sugar. When cool add the lemon juice, strong tea, pectolase and yeast nutrient. Introduce the activated wine yeast, and ferment on the "pulp" for 10 days, stirring the "must" twice daily with a wooden spoon and keep it closely covered. Then strain, for secondary fermentation, into a fermentation vessel and fit air-lock. Leave to ferment in the normal way, racking as necessary in due course.

Parsley and Balm

Ingredients:

1 lb. fresh parsley, including stalks (or $\frac{1}{2}$ packet dried parsley)
$\frac{1}{2}$ lb. fresh balm leaves (or $\frac{1}{3}$ packet dried balm leaves)
1 lb. raisins (or mixed dried fruit, currants, or sultanas, etc.)
2 ozs. dried bananas (optional) or dried rose hips/shells
3 lbs. sugar
$\frac{1}{2}$ pint strong tea (or a pinch of grape tannin)
1 level teaspoon citric acid (or 2 lemons, no pith, in lieu)
Water to finally make up 1 gallon of "must"
Yeast nutrient and activated wine yeast

Method:

Chop or bruise the herbs and place these with the chopped fruits and sugar into the initial fermentation vessel. Pour in the *boiling* water and stir well with a wooden spoon to dissolve the sugar. When cool add all the other ingredients. Ferment on the "pulp" for six days, then strain into fermentation jar, fit air-lock and ferment out, rack and bottle as usual.

Parsley and Carrot

Ingredients:

1 lb. parsley (fresh) or 1 packet dried parsley
3 lbs. carrots
$2\frac{1}{2}$ lbs. sugar
$\frac{1}{4}$ oz. citric acid (or 3 lemons, no pith, in lieu)
$\frac{1}{2}$ pint strong tea (or $\frac{1}{10}$ oz. grape tannin)
Yeast nutrient and activated wine yeast
Water: sufficient to finally produce 1 gallon of "must"

Method:

Scrape the young carrots and cut in two length-ways. Cook these 80% in four pints of water. Have ready *boiling* water in which to place the carrots after straining carrot essence on to sugar in the initial fermentation vessel. The carrots when transferred to the second vessel to which salt is added may then be finally cooked and eaten. In a separate vessel bring two pints of water to the boil and add the bruised and lightly chopped parsley. When this has boiled half a minute leave to infuse for one hour then strain into the sugared carrot essence. When cool add the acid, strong tea, yeast nutrient and activated wine yeast. Cover closely and ferment for three days, then transfer through nylon sieve to fermentation vessel and top up with water if necessary. Fit air-lock and ferment in normal way, racking as necessary in due course. A pleasant light, dry table wine.

Parsley and Rice

Ingredients:

1 lb. parsley (or small packet dried variety)
2lbs. paddy rice wite husks (or barley)
1lb. raisins (sultanas, figs, apricots, etc., may be used instead)
½ oz. citric acid (or 3 lemons, no pith, in lieu)
$\frac{1}{16}$ oz. grape tannin (or ½ pint strong tea)
3 lbs. sugar (or 4 lbs. honey)
Yeast nutrient and activated wine yeast
Water: sufficient to finally produce 1 gallon of "must"

Method:

Cut up the parsley into small pieces and place in the initial fermentation vessel together with the paddy rice, dried fruits and sugar. Pour in the *boiling* water and stir well to dissolve the sugar. When cool add the acid, tannin, yeast nutrient and introduce the activated wine yeast. Cover securely and leave to ferment for 10 days, then strain into fermentation bottles and fit air lock. Leave to ferment in normal way, racking in due course as necessary.

Variations:

1. 1 quart cider instead of dried fruit (to be added to "must" when cool).
2. Use ¼ bottle Vierka concentrated "must" instead of dried fruit—again add only to the "must" when cool.

Parsnip

Ingredients:

4 lbs. parsnips	1 lb. cleaned raisins
1 gallon and two pints water	2 oranges
	2 lemons
4 lbs. granulated sugar	Yeast and nutrient

Method:

Scrub and slice the parsnips and put into a large pan with six pints of the water. Bring to the boil and simmer for five minutes. Remove the scum as it rises. Strain through nylon sieve into a bowl and discard the "pulp." Add 2 lbs. of the sugar and stir until it is dissolved. Chop the raisins and cut the oranges and lemons into small pieces. Put them in parsnip mixture. When liquid is cool, add the yeast nutrient. Cover the bowl with polythene and leave ten days for the first fermentation. Strain through muslin into a bucket. Put 2 lbs. sugar into pan with four pints of water, bring to the boil and simmer for two minutes. Allow to cool, then stir into the liquor. Pour liquid through a funnel into a glass jar, fit a cork and lock and leave until second fermentation has ceased, rack and bottle wine.

Parsnip and Apricot

Ingredients:

4–6 lbs. parsnips
1 lb. dried apricots
1 or 2 pints commercial or home-made cider (or ¼ bottle Vierka concentrated "must")
3½ lbs. sugar
½ oz. citric acid (or 3 lemons, no pith, in lieu)
½ pint cold strong tea (or a pinch of grape tannin)
Water to make up 1 gallon "must"
Yeast nutrient and activated wine yeast

Method:

Simmer gently in half the water the scrubbed and thinly sliced parsnips, until slightly tender. Place the chopped apricots and sugar into the initial fermentation vessel: strain into this the hot parsnip liquor. Stir to dissolve the sugar. When cool add the cold tea or grape tannin and citric acid or lemon juice; add the cider and the remainder of the water to make up one gallon of "must." Add the yeast nutrient and then introduce the activated wine yeast. Ferment on the "pulp" for 10 days then strain into fermentation bottles. Fit air lock and leave to ferment in normal way, racking as necessary in due course.

Parsnip and Beetroot

Ingredients:

4 lbs. parsnips
2 lbs. beetroot
½ lb. or 1 lb. malt extract
½ pint cold strong tea
4 lbs. sugar
½ oz. citric acid (or 3 lemons, no pith, in lieu)
1 gallon water
Yeast nutrient and activated wine yeast

Method:

Wash the roots well—do not peel—slice thinly and simmer gently until slightly tender. Place the sugar and malt extract into a polythene bucket or crock vessel, then strain into this the hot liquor from the roots and stir until the sugar and malt is dissolved. When cool add the cold strong tea and citric acid. Then add the yeast nutrient and introduce the activated wine yeast. Cover well and three days later strain into fermentation vessels. Fit air-lock and leave to ferment in normal way, racking as necessary in due course.

Parsnip and Birch Sap

Ingredients:

> 3 lbs. parsnips
> ½ gallon of birch sap (see Birch Sap, p. 23)
> 1 lb. raisins (or other dried fruit)
> 2 ozs. dried rose hips/shells (or 2 ozs. dried bananas)
> 3 lbs. sugar or 4 lbs. invert sugar
> ¼ pint strong tea (or ½ teaspoonful grape tannin)
> ½ oz. citric acid (or 3 lemons, no pith, in lieu)
> Water to finally make up 1 gallon of "must"

Method:

Slice and simmer the old parsnips in four pints of water in the normal way. Place the chopped raisins, rose hips and half the sugar into the initial fermentation vessel and strain into this the hot parsnip liquor. Stir to dissolve the sugar. When cool (70°F.) add the chopped fruits, strong tea, citric acid, yeast nutrient, and introduce the activated wine yeast. Leave closely covered to ferment. In early March obtain ½ gallon of birch sap and heat this sufficiently to dissolve into it the balance of the sugar. When cool add this to the fermenting "must." After 10 days from commencement of fermentation, strain into secondary fermentation vessel. Fit air-lock and leave to ferment in the normal way, racking as necessary in due course.

Variations:

1. Sycamore and walnut sap can be used in lieu.

2. Place 24 bruised young birch leaves in the fermenting "must" if the lemon-like fragrance attached to birch wood is desired.

3. If insufficient birch sap is available make up the difference with cider.

The making of birch sap wine, together with illustrations of the tapping of a birch tree is also described in detail in "First Steps in Winemaking."

Parsnip and Date

Ingredients:

> 4–6 lbs. parsnips
> 2 lbs. dates
> 2 ozs. dried bananas
> 3 lbs. sugar
> ½ oz. citric acid (or 3 lemons, no pith, in lieu)
> ½ pint cold strong tea (or a pinch of grape tannin)
> Water to make up 1 gallon "must"
> Yeast nutrient and activated wine yeast

Method:

Scrub and slice thinly the parsnips and simmer gently in half the water until slightly tender. Place the chopped dates, dried bananas and sugar into a polythene or crock vessel for initial fermentation, then strain into this the hot parsnip liquor. Stir to dissolve the sugar. When cool add the cold tea or grape tannin and citric acid or lemon juice. Add the remainder of the water to make up the necessary amount of "must," then add the yeast nutrient and introduce the activated wine yeast. Ferment on the "pulp" for 10 days then strain into fermentation bottles. Fit air-lock and leave to ferment in normal way, racking as necessary in due course.

Parsnip and Elderflower

Ingredients:

4 lbs. parsnips

$\frac{1}{8}$ pint dried elderflowers

3 grapefruit

1 lb. raisins

3 lbs. sugar

1 tablespoon strong tea (or a $\frac{1}{2}$ teaspoon grape tannin)

$\frac{1}{2}$ oz. citric acid (or 3 lemons, no pith)

Water to finally produce 1 gallon of "must"

Yeast nutrient and activated wine yeast

Method:

Simmer gently in half the water the scrubbed and thinly sliced parsnips until slightly tender, avoid over-cooking and do not press out. Peel the grapefruit very thinly and discard the pith. Put the skins into the oven, and bake them until they are browned, then pour over them a quart of *boiling* water and infuse as in making tea. Place the sugar into the initial fermentation vessel and strain into this the hot parsnip liquor and stir to dissolve the sugar. When cool (70°F.) add the chopped raisins, pulped grapefruit, dried elderflowers and infusion from the grapefruit skins. Add the tea, citric acid, yeast nutrient and introduce the activated wine yeast. Ferment closely covered, for 10 days, then strain into the secondary fermentation vessel. Fit air-lock and leave to ferment in the normal way, racking as necessary in due course. Tinned grapefruit may be used in lieu of fresh fruit.

Parsnip and Fig

Ingredients:

4–6 lbs. parsnips
2 lbs. dried figs
2 ozs. dried rose hips/shells
3 lbs. sugar
Yeast nutrient and activated
    wine yeast

½ oz. citric acid (or 3
    lemons, no pith, in lieu)
½ pint cold strong tea (or a
    pinch of grape tannin)
Water to make up 1 gallon
    "must"

Method:

Scrub the parsnips (which are best lifted aftter the first frost) but do not peel. Cut into thin slices and simmer gently in half the / water until slightly tender. Place the cut up dried figs, rose hips (shells) and sugar into a polythene bucket or crock vessel, then strain into this the hot parsnip liquor. Stir to dissolve the sugar. When cool add the cold tea or grape tannin and citric acid or lemon juice. Add the remainder of the water to make up the necessary amount of "must," then add the yeast nutrient and introduce the activated wine yeast. Ferment on the "pulp" for 10 days, then strain into fermentation bottles. Fit air-lock and leave to ferment in normal way, racking as necessary in due course.

Parsnip and Orange

Ingredients:

3–4 lbs. parsnips
6–8 oranpes (see note below)
1½ lbs. raisins (or ¼ pint grape concentrate)
3 lbs. sugar (dry wine) or 4 lbs. sugar (sweet wine)
¼ pint strong tea (or ½ teaspoonful grape tannin)
½ oz. citric acid (or 3 lemons, no pith, in lieu)
Water to finally produce 1 gallon of "must"
Yeast nutrient and activated wine yeast

Method:

Scrub the parsnips (which are best lifted after the first frost) but do not peel. Cut into thin slices and simmer gently in half the water until slightly tender—avoid over boiling, otherwise difficulty may be experienced in clearing the wine. Peel the oranges very thinly and discard the pith. Put the skins into the oven, and bake them until they are browned then pour over them a quart of *boiling* water and infuse as in making tea. Place the sugar into the initial fermentation vessel and strain into this the hot parsnip liquor and stir to dissolve the sugar. When cool (70°F.) add the chopped raisins, pulped oranges and the infusion from the skins. Add the strong tea, citric acid, yeast nutrient and introduce the activated wine yeast. Ferment, closely covered, on the "pulp" for

10 days, then strain into the secondary fermentation vessel. Fit air-lock and leave to ferment in the normal way, racking later as necessary.

It is recognised generally that a mixture of varieties of Jaffa, Seville or sweet oranges and tangerines produce the most interesting results, but the use of one variety only is not detrimental to good results.

Parsnip and Rice

Ingredients:

> 4–6 lbs. parsnips
> 3 lbs. paddy rice, with husks (crushed maize, barley or wheat may be substituted)
> 1 lb. raisins or ½ pint grape concentrate
> 3 lbs. sugar
> ½ oz. ctiric acid (or 3 lemons, no pith, in lieu)
> ½ pint cold strong tea (or a pinch of grape tannin)
> Water to make up 1 gallon "must"
> Yeast nutrient and activated wine yeast

Method:

Scrub and thinly slice parsnips and simmer until slightly tender. Pour the parsnip liquor over the paddy rice, chopped raisins and sugar. Stir until sugar is dissolved and then when cool add the citric acid and cold tea. Introduce the activated wine yeast and yeast nutrient. Ferment on the "pulp" for 10 days, then strain into fermentation bottles. Fit air lock and leave to ferment in normal way, racking as necessary in due course.

Parsnip and Peach

Ingredients:

> 4 lbs. parsnips
> 1 tin peaches, or 1 lb. dried peaches (1 lb. 12 ozs. approx.)
> 2 lbs. bananas, including skins (or 2 ozs. dried bananas)
> 3 lbs. sugar
> A pinch of grape tannin
> ½ oz. citric acid (or 3 lemons, no pith, in lieu)
> ½ oz. Pectolase
> Water to produce finally 1 gallon "must"
> Yeast nutrient and activated wine yeast

Method:

Do not peel the parsnips but scrub them well and slice thinly. Simmer gently in water until slightly tender. Place the tinned peaches and syrup (chop up dried peaches if used), chopped bananas and sugar into the initial fermentation vessel and strain into this the hot parsnip liquor. Stir well to dissolve the sugar, etc. When cool (70°F.) add the tannin, citric acid or lemon juice, pectolase and yeast nutrient, and introduce the activated wine yeast. Cover closely, and leave to ferment for 10 days, stirring the "must" daily. Then strain into secondary fermentation vessel and fit air-lock. Leave to ferment in the normal way, racking in due course when necessary.

Parsnip and Pineapple

Ingredients:

4 lbs. parsnips
1 large or 2 small pineapples
1 lb. raisins (or other dried fruits)
3 lbs. sugar (or 4 lbs. honey)
½ teaspoonful grape tannin
The juice of 2 lemons
1 teaspoonful Pectolase
Water to make up 1 gallon of "must"
Yeast nutrient and activated wine yeast

Method:

Prepare the parsnip liquor in the normal way by *boiling* the sliced parsnips till tender, and straining. Place the chopped raisins, sugar and finely chopped pineapple into the initial fermentation vessel and pour in to this the hot parsnip liquor. Stir well to dissolve the sugar, etc. When cool (70°F.) add the tannin, lemon juice, pectolase and yeast nutrient; introduce the activated wine yeast. Cover securely and leave to ferment for 10 days, stirring each day. Then strain into secondary fermentation vessel and ferment under protection of an air-lock in the normal way, racking in due course as necessary.

Peach (dried)

Ingredients:

2 lbs. dried peaches	2½ lbs. sugar
1 gallon water	1 lemon
Yeast and nutrient	1 orange

Method:

Wash peaches and soak overnight in the gallon of water. Bring to the boil and simmer until tender. Strain off hot liquid into jar containing the sugar (and use cooked peaches for serving cold with cream). Add the orange and lemon, thinly sliced and stir. When cool add the yeast and stir thoroughly. Leave for 10 days, stirring daily. Strain off into jar and fit air-lock.

Pear

Ingredients:

4 lbs. pears

1 lb. raisins

3 lbs. sugar

1 gallon water

Yeast and nutrient

Method:

Cut up the pears and chop the raisins. Pour over them the water, *boiling*, and then dissolve in the mixture 2 lbs. of the sugar; stir well. Allow to cool to 70°F. before adding the yeast and nutrient. Cover closely, and allow to stand in a warm place for 10 days, stirring daily, then strain, add the remaining sugar to the liquor, and pour into fermenting jar. Fit air-lock and ferment in temperature of 60–65°F. for about three months; then siphon the wine off the lees into a clean jar. Refit lock and leave for a further two months before bottling.

Pear and Apple

Ingredients:

4 lbs. pears (really ripe ones)

4 lbs. mixed apples (eating, cooking and crab if possible)

1 lb. dried peaches (or apricots, figs, raisins, etc.)

2 ozs. dried rose hips/shells

3 lbs. sugar (or 4 lbs. honey)

½ oz. citric acid (or 3 lemons, no pith, in lieu)

Water to finally make up 1 gallon of "must"

Yeast nutrient and activated wine yeast

Method:

Grate up the pears and apples, including cores and skins. Chop up the dried fruits, and these place together with the sugar into the initial fermentation vessel. Pour in the *boiling* water and stir with a wooden spoon to dissolve the sugar, etc. When cool add the citric acid, grape tannin and yeast nutrient. Introduce the activated wine yeast and ferment on the "pulp" for 10 days, stirring the "must" with a wooden spoon twice daily, ensuring that the "must" is closely covered. Then strain, for secondary fermentation into fermentation vessel, and fit air-lock. Leave to ferment in the normal way, racking as necessary in due course.

"You always know when you've had enough—you start seeing hallucinations"

Pineapple and Grape

Ingredients:

1 tin pineapple (1 lb. 12 ozs. approx.)
1 pint concentrated grape juice (white)
½ teaspoonful citric acid or tartaric acid
⅛ pint strong tea
2½ lbs. sugar
Yeast nutrient and activated wine yeast
Water: sufficient to finally produce 1 gallon of "must"

Method:

Place the chopped pineapple and juice together with the grape concentrate in the initial fermentation vessel. Dissolve the sugar in hot water and add this to the fruit and grape concentrate. When cool (70°F.) add the strong tea, citric acid (or tartaric acid) and yeast nutrient. Introduce the activated wine yeast. Cover securely and leave to ferment for 10 days on the "pulp," stirring occasionally, then strain into the secondary fermentation vessel. Fit air-lock and leave to ferment in the normal way, racking later as necessary.

Variations:

1. 2 ozs. dried banana or 1 lb. fresh bananas including skins may be added.
2. Substitute 2 lbs. chopped raisins/sultanas for grape concentrate.

Plum

Ingredients:

3 lbs. plums   1 gallon water
½ lb. barley   Yeast and nutrient
3½ lbs. sugar

Method:

Grind the barley in a mincer or coffee grinder and cut up the fruit, putting both into a bowl. Pour over them the *boiling* water, cover closely, and leave for four days, giving a vigorous stir twice daily. Then strain through nylon sieve on to the sugar, add the yeast nutrient, and stir till all is dissolved. Add the yeast, preferably a Burgundy wine yeast, but failing that a general-purpose wine yeast or a level teaspoon of granulated yeast. Keep closely covered in a warm place for a week, then pour into fermenting bottle, filling to bottom of neck, and fit air-lock. Siphon off for the first time when it clears but do not bottle until assured that fermentation has completely finished.

Pomegranate

Ingredients:

8 large pomegranates
3 lbs. (plus) of sugar
1 gallon water

½ teaspoonful citric acid
½ oz. pectolase
G.P. wine yeast and nutrient

Method:

Take all the seeds out of the pomegranates, and remove the yellow skin. Press the pulp by hand in a muslin cloth and put the expressed juice into a bowl or polythene bucket. Boil up 2 lbs. of sugar in 4 pints of water and pour on to the juice. When cool add pectolase, nutrient, ½ teaspoon citric acid and G.P. wine yeast. Ferment in the warmth, covered, for seven days. Then boil up 1 lb. of sugar in 3 pints of water and put all into 1 gallon jar, fit airlock, and ferment on. When the S.G. drops below 1.020, feed it with small amounts of sugar. Final S.G. should be about 1.018.

Prune

Ingredients:

2 lbs. prunes
1 gallon water
½ lb. raisins, 1 lemon

3 lbs. sugar
Yeast and nutrient

Method:

Pour the cold water over the prunes and chopped raisins add a crushed Campden tablet, and let them stand for 10 days, stirring and mashing the fruit daily, then strain, being careful to extract all the liquid from the fruit before discarding it. Pour the liquor over the sugar, stir well to dissolve, add the juice of the lemon, and put the "must" into a fermenting jar (1 gallon). Add the yeast and yeast nutrient. Leave to ferment out (about two months) and rack into a clean jar when clear. Rack again after a further three months into clean bottles. This makes an excellent medium wine; for a dry wine reduce the sugar to 2½ lbs.

Prune and Rhubarb

Ingredients:

2 lbs. prunes
3 lbs. rhubarb
1 gallon cold water

3 lbs. sugar
Yeast and nutrient

Method:

Cut the rhubarb into small pieces and put it into a bowl with the prunes, and cover with the water, cold. Add one Campden tablet. After 24 hours add the yeast and nutrient, and stir in 1 lb. sugar. Ferment on the "pulp" for 10 days, mashing the fruit with the hands and giving it a good stir each day. On the seventh day stir in the remainder of the sugar, and on the 11th day strain the liquor into a fermenting jar and fit an air-lock. Press any juice out of the fruit, and include that, and also see to it that the 1 gallon jar is full, topping up with cold water if necessary. Ferment out, racking when the wine clears, and again 2–3 months later, this time into bottles.

Prune and Date

Ingredients:

1 lb. prunes
1 lb. dates
1 lb. sultanas (or raisins, currants, etc.)
½ oz. citric acid (or 3 lemons, no pith, in lieu)
½ pint strong tea (or a pinch of grape tannin)
2½ lbs. sugar (or 3 lbs. honey)
Water to finally make up 1 gallon of "must"
Yeast nutrient and activated wine yeast

Method:

Chop up the dried fruits and place these together with the sugar into the initial fermentation vessel. Pour in the *boiling* water and stir with a wooden spoon to dissolve the sugar, etc. When cool, add the strong tea, citric acid and yeast nutrient. Introduce the activated wine yeast and ferment on the "pulp" for 10 days, stirring the "must" with a wooden spoon twice daily, ensuring that the "must" is closely covered. Then strain, for secondary fermentation, into fermentation vessel, and fit air-lock. Leave to ferment in the normal way, racking as necessary in due course.

Prune and Grape Concentrate

Ingredients:

1 lb. dried prunes
1 pint grape concentrate (white or red)
4 ozs. dried rose hips/shells (or 3 ozs. dried bananas)
2½ lbs. sugar
¼ oz. citric acid (or 2 lemons, no pith)
¼ pint strong tea (or a pinch of grape tannin)
Yeast nutrient and activated wine yeast
Water: sufficient to finally produce 1 gallon of "must"

Method:

Place the chopped fruits and rose hips/shells and the sugar into the initial fermentation vessel and pour in the *boiling* water. Stir well with a wooden spoon to dissolve the sugar, then stir in the grape concentrate. When cool (70°F.) add the citric acid, strong tea, yeast nutrient, and introduce the activated wine yeast. Cover securely and leave to ferment for 10 days, then strain (by siphoning into a nylon strainer held in the funnel) into the secondary fermentation bottle and fit air-lock. Leave to ferment in the normal way, racking later as necessary.

Punches

ALE PUNCH

Ingredients:

2 pints ale	1 oz. sugar cubes
1 gill rum	3 cloves
1 gill gin	Nutmeg
1 gill whisky	Cinnamon
1 lemon/orange	1 pint water

Method:

Rub the sugar on the thinly pared (discard pith) lemon rind and place in a saucepan, to this add a pinch of cinnamon and a grating of nutmeg and the strained juice of the lemon, then add the ale, water, cloves and spirits. Stir and gently heat until quite hot—avoid *boiling*—serve hot with thin slices of orange or lemon on top.

FEATHERBED PUNCH

Ingredients:

3 glasses red wine	3 dessertspoons honey
1 glass whisky	¾ pint boiling water

Method:

Place the wine, honey and whisky in serving vessel and add the *boiling* water. Stir and serve. A half hot punch is half hearted so serve sizzling hot.

GINGER DELIGHT

Ingredients:

2 bottles ginger wine	1 small piece root ginger
2 ozs. sugar	1 pint water
2 eggs	1 lemon
4 cloves	

Method:

This is a favourite "non-alcoholic" warmer. Boil the cloves, thinly pared lemon rind and root ginger in one pint of water for 20 minutes. Add the ginger wine, sugar, and strained lemon juice. Heat up this mixture and pour half of it on to the beaten eggs. Whisk thoroughly and add the remainder of the mixture, and whisk once more. Serve hot and frothy.

GLOEGG (Swedish traditional Christmas drink)

Ingredients:

1 bottle red wine	1 stick cinnamon
2½ ozs. blanched almonds	10 cloves
¼ pint gin	5 ozs. seedless raisins

Method:

Place the ingredients, with the exception of the nuts and raisins, in the saucepan and heat to almost boiling point. Then remove the saucepan from the heat and add the nuts and raisins and allow these to soak for a few minutes. Serve hot in small glasses in which a spoon has been placed to enable the guests to fish out and eat the nuts and raisins.

HOT TODDY

Ingredients:

1 bottle medium sweet red wine	3 ozs. honey
1 small stick of cinnamon	1 lemon

Method:

Put the wine, honey and cinnamon in a saucepan and gently heat and add the thinly pared lemon rind and juice and serve hot.

HOT BLACKCURRANT PUNCH

Ingredients:

1 small tin blackcurrant purée	½ pint claret type wine
1 lemon	1–1½ pints water hot
½ pint sherry type wine	Sugar to taste

Method:

Place the thinly pared lemon rind (no pith) and lemon juice together with the pureé, claret and sherry type wines into a saucepan and heat slowly adding the sugar to suit your taste. Add water and heat up (avoid boiling). Remove rinds and serve in glasses with a slice of lemon.

HOT CUP (Eighteenth Century Classic mull)

Ingredients:

1 bottle red wine	12 lumps of sugar
1 wineglass of brandy	Grated nutmeg
1 wineglass of orange curacao	1 pint boiling water
6 cloves	

Method:

Place the sugar, cloves and wine into the saucepan and bring slowly to almost boiling then add the *boiling* water, brandy and curacao. Pour into glasses and sprinkle with grated nutmeg when serving.

PARTY CHEER

Ingredients:

1 bottle red wine	1 sherry glass liqueur
4 sticks of cinnamon	Sugar to taste
1 glass port wine	

Method:

Most simple to prepare. Just heat the mixture, avoiding boiling, and serve hot.

RUM PUNCH

This makes approximately 1 pint of punch—just enough to send the pair of you to bed comfortably on Christmas Eve!

Ingredients:

3 sherry glasses rum	2 tablespoonsful Demerara
3 sherry glasses white	sugar
country wine	1 sliced lemon
1 sherry glass of ginger wine	3 sherry glasses of water
Juice of 1 lemon	

Method:

Put sugar in small mixing bowl with lemon juice, add heated white wine and ginger wine, put in sliced lemon and stir. Now add rum and *boiling* water. Serve hot from bowl.

VIN CHAUD (Hot Wine)

Here it is, simple and cheap!

Ingredients:

1 bottle red wine	$\frac{1}{2}$ pint water
2 oranges	Grating of nutmeg
1 tablespoonful sugar	

Method:

Mix all the ingredients including the thinly pared rinds of the oranges—throw away pith—and place in a saucepan. Heat the mixture until it is very hot, avoid boiling. Pour into china mugs and drink as hot as possible—as should all Punches be drunk.

Quince

Ingredients:

24 quinces	2 lemons
½ lb. raisins	Yeast and nutrient
3 lbs. sugar	

Method:

Grate the quinces as near to the core as possible—a slow job, this—and boil the resultant pulp in the water for 15 minutes; then strain and throw the pulp away. Pour the liquid on to the sugar, and add the chopped raisins and the lemon juice. Stir well. Cool to 70°F. before adding the yeast and nutrient. Stand the bowl or polythene bucket in a warm place, covered closely with a cloth, for about 10 days, giving the liquor a thorough stirring daily. Then strain into a fermenting jar and fit air-lock. Leave in a temperature of 60–65°F. for about three months, then rack and proceed as usual. N.B. Be careful not to *over*boil the quince pulp or the wine will prove difficult to clear. This can be avoided by adding a tablespoon of pectolase to the liquid when it has cooled, and delaying the addition of the yeast and nutrient for 24 hours to allow the pectolase to do its work first.

Quince and Apricot

(A pleasant dessert wine with a heavy bouquet)

Ingredients:

2 lbs. (15 approx.) quinces
1 lb. dried apricots (or figs)
2 ozs. dried bananas (or 1 lb. fresh bananas including skins)
3 lbs. sugar (or 4 lbs. honey)
½ oz. citric acid (or 3 lemons, no pith, in lieu)
¼ oz. Pectolase
$\frac{1}{10}$ oz. grape tannin (or ½ pint strong tea)
Water to finally make up 1 gallon of "must"
Yeast nutrient and activated wine yeast

Method:

Grate the quinces and simmer the "pulp" for 15 minutes (avoid boiling otherwise the wine may not clear). Place the chopped fruits and sugar into the initial fermentation vessel, including chopped banana skins, if fresh bananas are used. Pour into this the hot liquor and quince pulp. Stir well with a wooden spoon to dissolve the sugar, etc. When cooled down to 70°F. add the citric acid, pectolase, grape tannin and yeast nutrient. Introduce the activated wine yeast and ferment on the "pulp" for 10 days, stirring each day, with a wooden spoon and ensuring the "must" is closely covered. Then strain into the secondary

"Now that's what I call full bodied, Harry"

fermentation vessel and leave to ferment under the protection of a fermentation lock, racking as necessary in due course.

Quince and Bilberry

Ingredients:

15 quinces (2 lbs. approx.)
½ lb. dried bilberries (or elderberries)
3 lbs. sugar (or 4 lbs. honey)
½ oz. citric acid (or 3 lemons, no pith, in lieu)
¼ oz. Pectolase
½ pint strong tea (or a pinch of grape tannin)
Water to finally make up 1 gallon of "must"
Yeast nutrient and activated wine yeast

Method:

Grate the quinces as near to the core as possible and simmer the "pulp" in water for 15 minutes (avoid exceeding this period). Place the dried bilberries and sugar into the initial fermentation vessel and pour into this the hot "pulp" and liquor. Stir well with a wooden spoon to dissolve the sugar, etc. When cooled down to 70°F. add the citric acid, pectolase, strong tea and yeast nutrient. Introduce the activated yeast and ferment for 10 days, stirring each day with a wooden spoon. Then strain into the secondary fermentation vessel and leave to ferment under the protection of a air-lock, racking as necessary in due course.

Red-currant

Ingredients:

4 lbs. red-currants
7 pints water
1 Campden tablet
3½ lbs. granulated sugar
Yeast and nutrient

Method:

Remove any stems from fruit and wash it well. Press it in a bowl with a wooden spoon. Bring four pints of the water to the boil and mix with the fruit. Crush the Campden tablet and mix with two tablespoons warm water. Add to the fruit. Cover bowl with polythene and leave to stand in a warm place for 24 hours, stirring occasionally. Strain mixture through muslin or nylon sieve into polythene bucket. Discard "pulp." Boil remaining three pints of water; dissolve sugar in it; pour syrup on to fruit.

When the water has cooled slightly, add yeast. Cover bucket with polythene and leave in a warm place for 10 days for the first fermentation. Pour wine into glass jar through funnel; fit cork and lock and leave until fermentation has stopped. Rack wine into bottles.

Red Dock

Ingredients:

    1 lb. red dock leaves
    1 lb. raisins (sultanas or currants, etc.)
    2 ozs. dried bananas
    3 lbs. sugar
    $\frac{1}{2}$ pint strong tea (or a pinch of grape tannin)
    $\frac{1}{2}$ oz. citric acid (or 3 lemons, no pith, in lieu)
    Water to finally make up 1 gallon of "must"
    Yeast nutrient and activated wine yeast

Method:

Shred the leaves and place these together with the chopped fruits and sugar into the initial fermentation vessel. Pour in the *boiling* water and stir well with a wooden spoon to dissolve the sugar. When cool add the citric acid, strong tea, and yeast nutrient. Introduce the activated wine yeast and ferment on the "pulp" for 10 days, stirring the "must" twice daily with a wooden spoon and keep it closely covered. Then strain, for secondary fermentation, into the fermentation vessel and fit air-lock. Leave to ferment in the normal way, racking as necessary in due course.

Red Table Wines

RECIPE 1

Ingredients:

10 lbs. elderberries	Nutrients
10 lbs. raisins	Beaujolais yeast starter
4 lbs. sugar	Water to $4\frac{1}{2}$ gallons

Method:

Crush the elderberries and strain off the juice. Leach the "pulp" by adding one gallon of *boiling* water, stirring for five minutes and then straining off the "pulp." Repeat this treatment with a second gallon of *boiling* water. Add the raisins and nutrients to this elderberry extract followed by another $1\frac{1}{2}$ gallons water. When cool add the yeast starter and ferment on the "pulp" for four days. Strain off the "pulp" and press lightly. Add the sugar, stir until completely dissolved and make up the volume to $4\frac{1}{2}$ gallons with water. Thereafter continue as usual with fermenting, racking and bottling.

RECIPE 2

Ingredients:

20 lbs. cherries	Nutrients
4 lbs. raisins	Pommard yeast starter
2 pints red grape concentrate	Water to 4½ gallons
4 lbs. sugar	

Method:

Add 3½ gallons *boiling* water to the washed cherries and raisins. Add the nutrients and sugar and stir until dissolved. When cool add the yeast starter. Ferment on the "pulp" until a sample drawn off from the bulk is sufficiently deep in colour. Strain off and press the "pulp" lightly. Add the grape concentrate and make the volume up to 4½ gallons with water. Thereafter proceed as usual.

RECIPE 3

Ingredients:

12 lbs. elderberries	Nutrients
5 lbs. greengages	Bordeaux yeast starter
2 pints red grape concentrate	Water to 4½ gallons
6 lbs. sugar	

Method:

Crush the elderberries and strain off the juice. Leach the "pulp" by adding one gallon *boiling* water, stirring for five minutes then straining off the "pulp." Repeat this procedure with a second gallon of *boiling* water. Add the stoned greengages, sugar, nutrients and another gallon of water to this elderberry extract and stir well until dissolved. When cool add the yeast starter. Ferment on the "pulp" for four days then strain off the "pulp" and press lightly. Add the grape concentrate and make the volume up to 4½ gallons with water. Thereafter proceed as usual.

RECIPE 4

Ingredients:

12 lbs. bilberries	Nutrients
10 lbs. peaches	Pommard yeast starter
2 pints red grape concentrate	Water to 4½ gallons
6 lbs. sugar	

Method:

Crush the bilberries and add the stoned peaches. Add 2½ gallons *boiling* water, sugar and nutrients and stir until dissolved. When cool add the yeast starter. Ferment on the "pulp" until a satisfactory depth of colour is attained then strain off the "pulp" and press lightly. Add the grape concentrate and sufficient water to make the volume up to 4½ gallons. Thereafter proceed as usual.

RECIPE 5

Ingredients:

25 lbs. dessert apples	Nutrients
12 lb. elderberries	Pommard yeast starter
2 pints red grape concentrate	Water to 4½ gallons
5 lbs. sugar	

Method:

Crush the elderberries and strain off the juice. Add one gallon *boiling* water to the pulp, stir for five minutes then strain off the "pulp." Repeat this treatment with a further gallon of boiling water. Add the elderberry juice and hot extracts to the washed sliced apples. Dissolve the sugar and nutrients in this solution. When cool add the yeast starter. Ferment on the "pulp" for seven days then strain off the "pulp" and press lightly. Add the grape concentrate and sufficient water to make the volume up to 4½ gallons. Thereafter proceed as usual.

RECIPE 6

Ingredients:

25 lbs. plums (red or blue)	Nutrients
4 lbs. raisins	Pommard yeast starter
4 pints red grape concentrate	Water to 4½ gallons
2 lbs. honey	1 oz. pectozyme

Method:

Wash and stone the plums and add the raisins and honey. Add three gallons *boiling* water and the nutrients. When cool add the pectozyme and yeast starter. Ferment on the "pulp" for five to six days then strain off the "pulp" and press lightly. Add the red grape concentrate and sufficient water to make the volume up to 4½ gallons. Thereafter proceed as usual.

RECIPE 7

Ingredients:

15 lbs. elderberries	Nutrients
6 lbs. bananas	Rhone or Burgundy yeast
2 pints red grape concentrate	starter
9 lbs. sugar	Water to 4½ gallons

Method:

Crush the elderberries and strain off the juice. Peel the bananas and cut into slices (discarding the skins). Boil the slices in one gallon water for half an hour then strain the hot liquor over the elderberry "pulp." Stir for five minutes then strain off the "pulp." Repeat this treatment with another gallon *boiling* water. Dissolve the sugar and nutrients in the combined extracts. When cool add the grape concentrate and make up the volume to 4½ gallons with water. Add the yeast starter. When the first violent fermentation has abated top up to 4½ gallons with water. Thereafter proceed as usual.

Rhubarb

Rhubarb contains an excess of oxalic acid, which is rather unpleasant, and is best removed by the use of precipitated chalk. Rhubarb picked mid-May is best for winemaking.

Ingredients:

5 lbs. rhubarb stalks	1 gallon water
3½ lbs. preserving sugar	Precipitated chalk
Yeast	Yeast nutrient
	Juice of 2 lemons

Method:

Wipe the rhubarb clean, but do not peel, and chop into short lengths. Pour the *boiling* water over it, allow it to become cold, then strain off the liquor and add to it the juice pressed from the stalks. To this add 1 oz. of precipitated chalk and stir well in. This may suffice, but if the juice still has an acid taste, add up to another ½ oz. Then put in the sugar, stirring well until all is dissolved, add the juice pressed out of two large lemons, and put in the yeast. Put into fermenting vessel and fit air-lock, keeping half a pint or so separately in a bottle plugged with cotton wool for "topping up" when the ferment quietens. Leave until the wine clears, then siphon off for the first time. If you wish to remove all colour add half a dozen clean, broken eggshells.

Rhubarb and Centaury

Ingredients:

4 llbs. rhubarb
1 packet centaury herb
   or ½ lb. fresh herb (the whole herb is used)
1 lb. raisins (or other dried fruit)
3½ lbs. sugar
½ pint strong tea (or a pinch of grape tannin)
½ oz. citric acid (or 3 lemons, no pith, in lieu)
Sufficient water to finally produce 1 gallon "must"
Yeast nutrient and activated wine yeast

Method:

Having extracted the rhubarb juice by the cold water method, using precipitated chalk to remove excess oxalic acid, place the herb in a boiler and simmer in the remainder of the water cutting off the heat at *boiling* point. Leave to infuse for three hours. Place the chopped fruit and sugar in the initial fermentation vessel. Bring the herb liquor up to *boiling* point, then strain into fermentation vessel, stirring to dissolve the sugar. When cool add the rhubarb juice, strong tea, citric acid, yeast nutrient and introduce the activated wine yeast. Ferment, closely covered for 10 days, then siphon into fermentation bottle. Fit air-lock and leave to ferment in normal way, racking as necessary. The herb is a bitter tonic and produces an "appetiser" type wine.

Rhubard and Bilberry

Ingredients:

4 lbs. rhubarb
½ lb. dried bilberries or elderberries (¼ lb. of each, together, may also be used)
1 lb. raisins or other dried fruit
3 lbs. sugar
½ pint strong tea (or a pinch of grape tannin)
½ oz. citric acid
Sufficient water to finally produce 1 gallon of "must"
Yeast nutrient and activated wine yeast

Method:

Using half the water, prepare the rhubarb by the cold water method, removing excess oxalic acid by using precipitated chalk—extraction by hot water may cause jellification; place the chopped raisins and other fruits together with the sugar in the initial fermentation vessel and pour over the remainder of the water, *boiling* hot. Stir well to dissolve the sugar. When cool add the prepared rhubarb juice, strong tea, citric acid, yeast nutrient and introduce the activated wine yeast. Ferment, closely covered, for 10 days, then strain into fermentation bottle. Fit air-lock and leave to ferment in the normal way, racking as necessary.

Rhubarb and Chervil Root

Ingredients:

3–4 lbs. rhubarb
2 lbs. chervil root (carrots may be substituted)
3½ lbs. sugar
¼ pint strong tea (or a pinch of grape tannin)
½ oz. citric acid (or 3 lemons, no pith, in lieu)
Sufficient water to finally produce 1 gallon "must"
Yeast nutrient and activated wine yeast

Method:

Extract the rhubarb juice by the cold water method using precipitated chalk. Boil the chervil roots or carrots until slightly tender in the remainder of the water. Place the sugar in the initial crock bowl and strain in the root juice, and stir to dissolve the sugar. When cool add the citric acid, strong tea, rhubarb juice,

107

yeast nutrient and introduce the activated wine yeast. Keep closely covered and ferment for 48 hours. Strain into fermentation bottle. Fit air-lock and leave to ferment in the normal way, racking in due course. Chervil roots can be cooked and served the same way as carrots. Roots for storing should be lifted in August.

Rhubarb and Chervil Flower

Ingredients:

> 3–4 lbs. rhubarb
> 2 pints chervil flower heads (or flower heads and leaves combined). (The root if lifted can be cooked and eaten as carrots)
> $3\frac{1}{2}$ lbs. sugar
> $\frac{1}{2}$ pint strong tea (or a pinch of grape tannin)
> $\frac{1}{2}$ oz. citric acid (or 3 lemons, no pith, in lieu)
> Sufficient water to finally produce 1 gallon "must"
> Yeast nutrient and activated wine yeast

Method:

Prepare the rhubarb juice by the cold water method using precipitated chalk to remove excess oxalic acid. Infuse the flower heads/leaves, etc., by simmering in remainder of the water cutting off heat at boiling point. Leave to infuse for three hours, then bring back to boiling point and strain on to sugar in initial fermentation vessel. Stir well to dissolve sugar and when cool add the rhubarb juice, strong tea, citric acid, yeast nutrient and activated wine yeast. Ferment, closely covered for 48 hours, then transfer to fermentation jars. Fit air-lock and leave to ferment in the normal way, racking in due course. This herb has a flavour of caraway and anise and blends well with the other ingredients.

Rhubarb and Ginger

Ingredients:

> 4 lbs. rhubarb
> 2 ozs. root ginger (or powdered ginger)
> 1 lb. raisins (or other dried fruit)
> $\frac{1}{2}$ lb. oak leaves (2 quarts) (or $\frac{1}{2}$ lb. tips of young blackberry shoots)
> 3 lbs. sugar
> $\frac{1}{2}$ pint strong tea (or a pinch of grape tannin)
> $\frac{1}{2}$ oz. citric acid (or 3 lemons, no pith, in lieu)
> Sufficient water to finally produce 1 gallon "must"
> Yeast nutrient and activated wine yeast

"A Campden tablet, please, waiter"

Method:

Use cold water extraction method and precipitated chalk to prepare the rhubarb juice. Place the washed shoots or leaves in the boiler and simmer in the remainder of the water, cutting off heat when at *boiling* point. Leave to infuse for three hours, then bring back to *boiling* point. Place the chopped fruit, crushed ginger and sugar into initial fermentation vessel and pour in the strained extract of the leaves or shoots. Stir well to dissolve the sugar. When cool add the rhubarb juice, strong tea, citric acid, yeast nutrient and introduce the activated wine yeast. Leave closely covered for 10 days, then siphon in fermentation jar. Fit air-lock, and leave to ferment in normal way, racking as necessary.

Rhubarb and Hawthorn Blossom

Ingredients:

3–4 lbs. rhubarb
$\frac{1}{4}$ lb. Hawthorn Blossom (May blossom) (or 1 quart blossom)
2 ozs. dried bananas
$3\frac{1}{2}$ lbs. sugar
$\frac{1}{2}$ pint strong tea (or a pinch of grape tannin)
$\frac{1}{2}$ oz. citric acid (or 3 lemons, no pith, in lieu)
Sufficient water to finally produce 1 gallon of "must"
Yeast nutrient and activated wine yeast

Method:

Prepare the rhubarb by the cold water extraction method and by using precipitated chalk to remove excess oxalic acid. Place the blossoms, fruit and sugar in the initial fermentation vessel and pour in the remainder of the water *boiling* hot, then stir to dissolve the sugar. When cool, add the rhubarb juice, strong tea, citric acid, yeast nutrient and introduce the activated wine yeast. Leave, closely covered, to ferment for seven days, then strain into fermentation jar. Fit air-lock and leave to ferment in the normal way, racking as necessary.

Rhubarb and Nettle

Ingredients:

3–4 lbs. rhubarb
$\frac{1}{2}$ lb. young nettle tops (2 quarts)
$\frac{1}{4}$ lb. dried rose hips/shells
1 lb. raisins (or other dried fruit)
3 lbs. sugar
$\frac{1}{2}$ pint strong tea (or a pinch of grape tannin)
$\frac{1}{2}$ oz. citric acid (or 3 lemons, no pith, in lieu)
Sufficient water to finally produce 1 gallon "must"
Yeast nutrient and activated wine yeast

Method:

Prepare the rhubarb by the cold water extraction method and use precipitated chalk. Wash and drain the young nettle tops and simmer these in the remainder of the water. Bring the water to *boiling* point then cut off heat and leave to soak for three hours and re-heat to almost boiling point. Place the rose hips, chopped dried fruit and sugar into the initial fermentation vessel and strain in the hot nettle extract. Stir well to dissolve the sugar. When cool add the rhubarb juice, strong tea, citric acid, yeast nutrient and lastly the activated wine yeast. Leave closely covered for 10 days then siphon into fermentation jar. Fit air-lock and leave to ferment in normal way, racking as necessary. In the initial stages of fermentation the nttle gives off a very strong odour—this need cause no concern as it does not persist.

Rhubarb and Clover

Ingredients:

3–4 lbs. rhubarb

$\frac{3}{4}$ lb. purple clover blossom ($\frac{3}{4}$ gallon flower heads)

1 lb. raisins (or other dried fruit)

$\frac{1}{2}$ oz. citric acid (or 3 lemons, no pith, in lieu)

$\frac{1}{2}$ pint strong tea (or a pinch of grape tannin)

3 lbs. sugar

Sufficient water to finally produce 1 gallon of "must"

Yeast nutrient and activated wine yeast

Method:

Wipe the rhubarb clean with a damp cloth. Do not peel, then cut into lengths and crush with a mallet, or pulper, or put through the domestic wringer! (enclosing the rhubarb in a muslin cloth) to extract as much juice as possible. Leave the juice and "pulp" in the crock and add one Campden tablet, then add half a gallon of cold water and leave this to soak, closely covered, for three days, stirring several times each day. Strain into fermentation jar, then add half ounce of precipitated chalk (obtainable from the chemist). Fit air-lock and leave for 24 hours, then siphon into a clean jar, being most careful not to distrub residue from the bottom of the jar. When this has been completed place the blossoms (flower heads), the chopped raisins and sugar into the initial fermentation vessel and pour in half gallon *boiling* water and stir to dissolve the sugar. When cool add the treated rhubarb juice, citric acid, strong tea, yeast nutrient and lastly the activated wine yeast. Leave to ferment with the solids, for seven days, closely covered. Strain into fermentation jar. Fit air-lock and leave to ferment in the normal way, racking as necessary.

Rhubarb and Spruce

Ingredients:

>4 lbs. rhubarb
>¼ oz. essence spruce (or a T. Noirot Extract to your own choice)
>4 lbs. sugar
>½ pint strong tea (or a pinch of grape tannin)
>½ oz. citric acid (or 3 lemons, no pith, in lieu)
>Sufficient water to finally produce 1 gallon of "must"
>Yeast nutrient and activated wine yeast

Method:

Using half the water, prepare the rhubarb by the cold water method, using precipitated chalk, which costs a few pence from any chemists' store. Use of hot water may cause jellification. Heat the remainder of the water and place the sugar in the initial fermentation vessel and pour in the hot water. Stir to dissolve the sugar. When cool add the rhubarb juice, strong tea, citric acid and nutrient, and then introduce the activated wine yeast. Ferment, closely covered, for two days, then transfer to fermentation bottles. Add the essence of extract and fit air-lock. Leave to ferment in the normal way, racking later as necessary.

Rice

Ingredients:

>1 lb. coarsely crushed rice   1 gallon water
>1 lb. minced raisins   Yeast and nutrient
>3 lbs. sugar

Method:

Pour *boiling* water on to the rice, sugar, raisins and thinly peeled skin of the lemon. Stir well and cover. When cool (70°F.) add the lemon juice, nutrient and yeast, and ferment all together for one week, stirring twice daily and keeping the crock or polythene bucket well covered. Strain into fermenting jar (without pressing) and ferment out. Rack when clear, and again two months later into clean bottles.

Rose Hip

Ingredients:

>2½ lbs. fresh rose hips   3 lbs. sugar
>   (or 6–8 oz. bottle rosehip   1 tablespoon pectolase
>   syrup)   1 gallon water
>1 lemon   Yeast and yeast nutrient

Method:

The easiest way to crush the rosehips is to run them through an ordinary domestic mincer with the outer cutting disc removed. The inner disc has holes just too small to allow them to pass freely and they are neatly crushed in the process (crushing them with a mallet or rolling pin, as sometimes recommended, is a tedious and sticky business). Pour over them the water, *boiling*. Allow to cool to 70°F., then add the pectolase and stir well in. Leave for 24 hours, covered with a cloth, then add the sugar, stirring well to dissolve it, a general purpose wine yeast, nutrient, and the juice of the lemon. Keep in a warm place, about 70°F., closely covered, for five or six days, stirring vigorously once a day. By then the fermentation will have quietened a little, so strain the liquor into a fermentation jar and fit an air-lock. Rack and bottle in the usual way. This is a strong-flavoured wine, high in alcohol, and some may prefer to sweeten it a little after it is made.

Rose Hip (dried)

Ingredients:

13 ozs. dried rose hips
2½ lbs. sugar
Juice of 1 lemon

Tokaier yeast and yeast
nutrient
1 gallon water

Method:

Dried rose hips can now be purchased in this country and one can thus avoid the tedious business of picking fresh hips. The dried ones make a wine fully as good, and rose hip wine *is* good, indeed the Germans hold that it is second only to the grape for winemaking. With the dried rose hips, which have been largely dehydrated, and therefore weigh less, a smaller quantity is required than when one uses the fresh fruit. Prepare your yeast starter two days before making the wine and soak the rose hips overnight in one pint of water. Mince your rose hips through an ordinary domestic mincer with the outer cutting disc removed and put into a bowl with the sugar and lemon juice. Pour over them the water, *boiling*. Stir well to dissolve the sugar. When the mixture has cooled to 70°F., add your fermenting Tokaier yeast. Cover closely with a polythene sheet secured by elastic and stand in a warm place (about 70°F.) but stir daily. After 10 days, strain into a one-gallon jar, topping up with cold boiled water to the bottom of the neck if necessary, and fit air-lock. When the wine clears rack into a clean jar and refit lock. Leave for a further three months, then rack into clean bottle and cork down.

113

Rose Hip Fig

(A dry white wine)

This is an adaptation by A. S. Henderson of a Vierka recipe, using rose hip syrup instead of rose hip shells. The original recipe is to produce a mock Tokay, the popular Hungarian wine, but this version produced a dry white wine almost identical to a good Liebfraumilch at 24/6 a bottle, he says.

Ingredients:

> 1 small bottle of Delrose rosehip syrup
> 4 ozs. figs
> 1 teaspoon citric acid
> 3½ lbs. sugar
> 9 pints water
> 1 Vierka Tokay yeast; nutrient

Method:

Wash the figs well, chop well, and put them in a polythene bucket with the sugar. Pour in a gallon of *boiling* water. Allow to cool, then add citric acid, yeast and nutrient, cover closely and ferment for about a week, closely covered. Strain through muslin or sieve into a fermentation jar, adding the rose hip syrup dissolved in any convenient amount of warm "must," a little at a time. Fit air-lock and ferment out in a warm place (about four to five weeks).

Rosemary and Carrot

Ingredients:

> 2 oz. packet of dried rosemary herb or 1 lb. fresh herb
>   (Rosemary Officinalis)
> 4 lbs. old carrots (turnips or swedes)
> 1 lb. figs or raisins
> 2½ lbs. sugar
> Juice of 2 lemons
> $\frac{1}{10}$ oz. grape tannin
> Water to finally make up 1 gallon of "must"
> Yeast nutrient and activated wine yeast

Method:

Scrub the carrots and chop them up, put them in the water and bring to the boil. Simmer until tender. Place the chopped fruit, sugar and herb into the initial fermentation vessel and strain into this the hot carrot liquor (the carrots may be eaten) and stir well to dissolve the sugar, etc. When cool (70°F.) add the citric acid and yeast nutrient. Introduce the activated yeast and ferment for 10 days, stirring every day with a wooden spoon. Then strain into secondary fermentation vessel and leave to ferment under the protection of an air-lock, racking as necessary in due course.

"I don't feel too happy about this Judge"

Rose Petal and Concentrate

Ingredients:

> 2 quarts strongly scented petals
> ¼ bottle Vierka Concentrated Must
>   (or 1 pint grape concentrate)
> ½ oz. citric acid (or 2 lemons, no pith, in lieu)
> ½ pint strong tea (or $\frac{1}{10}$ oz. grape tannin)
> 3 lbs. sugar (2½ lbs. of grape concentrate if used)
> Yeast nutrient and activated wine yeast
> Water: sufficient to finally produce 1 gallon of "must"

Method:

Use any rose petals—different varieties will produce a wine of differing bouquet. Place the petals in the initial fermentation vessel and pour over half of the water, *boiling* hot, cover securely and leave to infuse for two to three days, stirring daily. Then strain and place the rose scented extract back in the initial fermentation vessel and add the sugar. Pour over this the remainder of the water, *boiling* hot, and stir well to dissolve the sugar. When cool add the concentrate, acid, tannin, nutrient, and introduce the activated wine yeast. Cover well and leave to ferment three days, then transfer to fermentation bottles and fit air-lock. Leave to ferment in the normal way, racking as necessary, in due course.

Variations:

1. Use 4 lbs. honey in lieu of sugar.
2. Or add, instead of concentrates, a small bottle of black-currant juice or fresh juice from soft fruits, such as raspberries, etc.

Rose Petal and Peach

Ingredients:

> 2 quarts rose petals (strongly scented are preferrred)
> 2½ lbs. peaches (or 1 lb. dried peaches)
> 3 lbs. sugar
> 1 level teaspoon citric acid (or 2 lemons, no pith, in lieu)
> ½ pint strong tea (or a pinch of grape tannin)
> Water to finally make 1 gallon of "must"
> Yeast nutrient and activated wine yeast

Method:

Place the rose petals, stoned peaches (chop up the dried ones) and sugar into the initial fermentation vessel. Pour in the *boiling* water and stir well with a wooden spoon until the sugar is dissolved. When cool add the citric acid, strong tea and yeast nutrient.

Introduce the activated wine yeast and ferment on the "pulp" for 10 days, stirring the "must" twice daily with a wooden spoon and keep it closely covered. Then strain, for secondary fermentation, into a fermentation vessel and fit air-lock. Leave to ferment in the normal way, racking as necessary in due course.

Rowanberry

Ingredients:

1 quart rowanberries	½ lb. wheat
1 gallon water	2 tablespoons raisins (heaped)
3 lbs. sugar	Yeast and nutrient

Method:

This makes an excellent medium-sweet table wine, but if you wish to make a dry one cut the sugar to 2½ lbs. Pour the *boiling* water over the rowanberries, and let them stand for five days, stirring and mashing with the hand daily. Then strain the liquid on to the sugar, chopped raisins, and wheat, and stir well to dissolve the sugar. Add the yeast and nutrient (a general purpose) wine yeast starter or a level teaspoon of granulated yeast, and stand in a warm place, closely covered, for a further 10 days. Then strain into fermenting jar, fit air-lock, and leave until fermentation is finished and wine is clear. Then rack into clean jar. Bottle after a further three months.

Sage

Ingredients:

8 lbs. stoned raisins
1 lb. barley (if desired, it will lend "body" to the wine)
3 lbs. sage leaves
2 lemons
Yeast and nutrient
1 gallon water

Method:

Pour the *boiling* water on to the minced raisins and barley and add the chopped leaves of the red sage. Allow to cool and then add the juice of the two lemons and the yeast (a prepared wine yeast or a level teaspoonful of granulated yeast). Keep covered, in a warm place, for seven days, stirring daily, then strain into a fermentation vessel with an air-lock and ferment in the usual way. Alternatively, and more cheaply, the wine can be made by substituting 1 lb. raisins and 2½ lbs. sugar for the 8 lbs. of raisins.

Sage and Parsley

Ingredients:

1 lb. fresh parsley (or 2 ozs. dried parsley)
1 lb. sage (or 2 ozs. dried red sage)
1 lb. raisins (or sultanas, peaches, apricots, etc.)
2 ozs. dried bananas (1 lb. fresh bananas including skins)
3 lbs. sugar (or 4 lbs. honey)
$\frac{1}{4}$ oz. citric acid
1 tablespoon strong tea
Water to finally make up 1 gallon of "must"
Yeast nutrient and activated wine yeast

Method:

Chop up the parsley, sage, raisins and bananas. Place these into the initial fermentation vessel together with the sugar. Pour in the *boiling* water and stir with a wooden spoon to dissolve the sugar. When cool add the citric acid, strong tea, and yeast nutrient. Introduce the activated wine yeast and ferment on the "pulp" for 10 days, stirring the "must" with a wooden spoon twice daily; otherwise keep it closely covered. Then strain, for secondary fermentation into fermentation vessel, and fit air-lock. Leave to ferment in the normal way, racking as necessary in due course.

Sarsaparilla

Ingredients:

1 lb. Sarsaparilla leaves
$\frac{1}{2}$ lb. chopped raisins
3 lbs. sugar
2 lemons (or citric acid)
Yeast nutrient
Yeast (selected wine)

Method:

Pour the *boiling* water over the sarsaparilla leaves, chopped raisins and sugar. When cool add lemon juice or citric acid and the juice from the boiled lemon peel (no pith). Stir in yeast nutrient and activated wine yeast and ferment on the solids for six days, stirring daily. Then strain in fermentation glass jar. Fit air-lock and ferment in normal way.

Note: The sarsaparilla leaves are stocked by most herbalists and wine supplies' firms.

Sloe

Ingredients:

3 lbs. sloes (as ripe as possible)
3 lbs. sugar
1 gallon water
Burgundy yeast and nutrient

Method:

Bring the water to the boil and pour it over the sloes, crushing and breaking them as much as possible, then dissolve 2 lbs. of sugar in the liquid. Allow the mixture to cool to 70°F., before adding yeast starter (a Burgundy or Port yeast is excellent, failing that a general purpose yeast) and some yeast nutrient. Put the bowl or polythene bucket in a warm place (about 70°F.) and cover closely; ferment thus for about five days, stirring well each day. Strain, add the remaining 1 lb. of sugar to the juice, and pour into fermenting jar, filling to the bottom of the neck. Top up with a little cold boiled water if necessary. After about three months (temperature preferably 60–65°F.) there will be a yeast deposit, so rack into a clean jar and refit trap. Leave until wine is really clear, then rack into clean bottles and cork down.

Sloe and Apricot

Ingredients:

2 lbs. sloes

1 lb. dried apricots (or figs)

2 ozs. dried rose hips or rose hip shells

½ lb. raisins or sultanas

3 lbs. sugar

¼ oz. Pectolase

Juice of 2 lemons

¼ pint strong tea

Water to make up finally 1 gallon of "must"

Yeast nutrient and activated wine yeast

Method:

Break open the sloes and place together with the chopped dried fruits, hips and sugar into the initial fermentation vessel. Pour in the *boiling* water and stir well with a wooden spoon to dissolve the sugar and mash the fruits. When cooled down to 70°F. add the citric acid, Pectolase, strong tea and yeast nutrient. Introduce the activated wine yeast and ferment on the "pulp" for 10 days, stirring each day with a wooden spoon and ensuring the "must" is closely covered. Then strain into the secondary fermentation vessel, and leave to ferment under the protection of an air-lock, racking as necessary in due course.

119

Strawberry and Red-currant

Ingredients:

3 lbs. strawberries
1 lb. red-currants (or white-currants)
2 ozs. dried bananas (or 3 ozs. dried rose hips/shells)
½ oz. citric acid (or 3 lemons, no pith, in lieu)
½ pint strong tea (or $\frac{1}{10}$ oz. grape tannin)
½ oz. Pectolase
¾ oz. glycerine (B.P. quality)
3 lbs. sugar (or 4 lbs. honey)
Yeast nutrient and selected wine yeast
Water: sufficient to finally produce 1 gallon of "must"

Method:

Place the strawberries and red-currants in the initial fermentation vessel and macerate these with a wooden spoon, add the dried fruit and sugar. Pour over these the *boiling* water and stir well to dissolve the sugar. When cool add the acid, tannin, pectolase, yeast nutrient and introduce the activated wine yeast. Secure well and leave to ferment for 10 days, then strain into fermentation bottles, add the glycerine and fit air-lock. Leave to ferment in normal way, racking in due course as necessary. Avoid mouldy, damaged or overripe fruit.

Variations:

1. Use ½ lb. malt extract in lieu of dried bananas.
2. Or ¼ bottle of Vierka Concentrated Must (this should be added when the original "must" is cool).

Tea

Ingredients:

4 pints tea (saved left-overs)
1½ lbs. sugar
2 lemons
½ lb. raisins (large and chopped)
1 teaspoonful granulated yeast

Method:

The key to this most useful, easy-to-make wine is—6 ozs. of sugar to every pint of tea, as you can see from the above. Add the tea, which can be saved a little at a time until you have the required quantity, to the sugar and lemon juice and stir until dissolved. Pour into fermenting jar with yeast and chopped raisins, work out, and rack off when clear. Add amounts of yeast and nutrient (standing). A dry wine of a golden colour, and of not to strong a flavour. Excellent for blending purposes.

Turnip

Ingredients:

4 lbs. turnips	1 orange
3 lbs. sugar	Yeast and yeast nutrient
1 lemon	1 gallon water

Method:

Scrub the roots well—it is not necessary to peel them—and cut them into slices (¾″). Put them into a large saucepan or boiler in as much of the water as possible (leaving the remainder of the gallon to one side) bring to the boil, and simmer until the turnips are tender. Do not, however, allow them to go mushy or the wine may not clear. Strain off the liquor on to the remaining water, return it to the boiler, and add the sliced fruit and sugar. Simmer for half an hour, stirring well for the first few minutes, then strain through a nylon sieve or two thicknesses of muslin into a bowl or jar, and make it up to the gallon once more. Allow the liquor to cool to 70°F., then add your yeast (a wine yeast or ¾ oz. baker's yeast) and nutrient, and stir well. Cover bowl closely and leave for four days in a warm place (about 70°F.), then lower temperature and after three months the wine should be clearing and can be racked, or siphoned into a clean bottle, leaving the sediment behind. Again fit an air-lock. Leave for a further three months; then rack it again, this time into the wine bottles and cork securely.

Veitchberry

Ingredients:

4 lbs. veitchberries (a hybrid between a large blackberry and raspberry)
1 pint home-made or commercial cider (or ¼ bottle Vierka Concentrated Must)
3 lbs. sugar
Juice of 1 large lemon
¼ oz. Pectolase
Water to finally make up 1 gallon of "must"
Yeast nutrient and activated wine yeast

Method:

Place the berries into the initial fermentation vessel and add the sugar. Pour in the *boiling* water. Macerate and stir well with a wooden spoon to break up the berries and to dissolve the sugar. When cool add the cider or concentrated "must," lemon juice. Pectolase and yeast nutrient. Introduce the activated wine yeast and ferment on the "pulp" for 10 days, stirring the "must" twice daily with a wooden spoon, and keep it closely covered. Then strain, for secondary fermentation, into fermentation vessel and fit air-lock. Leave it to ferment in the normal way, racking as necessary in due course. (Blackberries and raspberries may be used in lieu of veitchberries.)

121

Vine Prunings

In the summer you are pruning your vines to keep them under control—each shoot should be pinched out leaving one leaf beyond each cluster of grape flowers and as the summer goes on you are likely to have plenty of prunings. Do not waste these, for they will make excellent wine. Here is a good recipe for a wine from a white grape vine such as Seyve Villard:

Ingredients:

8 pints boiling water	**Juice of one lemon**
4–5 lbs. leaves and tendrils	**Yeast and nutrient**
3 lbs. white sugar	

Method:

Chop the leaves, stems and tendrils—use a pair of secateurs—put them into a receptacle and pour over them the *boiling* water. Let this stand for 48 hours, but turn occasionally to submerge top leaves and keep prunings well under water (there will be only just enough water). Keep closely covered. Pour off liquid and press out leaves; if you have no press wring them in your hands. Wash the leaves with a pint of water and press again. Dissolve the sugar in the liquid, add the yeast, yeast nutrient and acid, pour into fermenting jar, and make up to one gallon with water. Fit air-lock. Ferment right out in the usual way and siphon off when clear.

Wheat

Ingredients:

1 pint wheat	**3½ lbs. demerara sugar**
2 lbs. raisins	**1 gallon water**
2 lemons	**Yeast**
1 orange	

Method:

Put the wheat (crushed through a mincer) and chopped raisins into a crock, together with the lemon rinds (no white pith), the fruit juice, and the sugar. Cover with *boiling* water and leave till cool, stirring at intervals. Add yeast and leave well covered in a warm place until vigorous fermentation has ceased. Strain into fermenting jar and fit air-lock, keep for about four months, and then siphon off into clean bottles. Leave at least six months before drinking. This is an excellent full-bodied sweet wine.

White-currant

Ingredients:

> 4 lbs. white-currants (or white elderberries when available)
> 1 lb. raisins (or other dried fruit)
> 2 ozs. dried bananas
> 3 lbs. sugar
> ½ oz. citric acid (or 3 lemons, no pith, in lieu)
> ½ pint strong tea (or a pinch of grape tannin)
> ¼ oz. Pectolase
> Water to finally make up 1 gallon "must"
> Yeast nutrient and activated wine yeast

Method:

Place the fruits and sugar into the initial fermentation vessel and pour in the *boiling* water. Macerate and stir well with a wooden spoon to break up the fruits and to dissolve the sugar. When cool add the citric acid, strong tea, pectolase and yeast nutrient. Introduce the activated wine yeast and ferment on the "pulp" for 10 days, stirring the "must" twice daily with a wooden spoon and keep it closely covered. Then strain, for secondary fermentation, into a fermentation vessel and fit air-lock. Leave to ferment in the normal way, racking as necessary in due course.

White Wine

(Vin Ordinaire)

Ingredients:

> ¼ pint canned orange juice
> ½ pint canned pineapple juice
> 2 lbs. sugar
> 1 teaspoonful Pectolase or equivalent
> Bordeaux yeast
> Water to 1 gallon

Method:

The sugar is poured into a gallon jar, the juices and nutrients, etc., are added and the jar is topped up to the shoulder with cold water. Vigorous stirring will dissolve the sugar and the yeast starter and pectolase are added immediately. This wine will ferment out to dryness in about three to four weeks at 75°F. At the end of this time two Campden tablets should be added and the wine racked a week later. After three to four months the wine is brilliantly clear and is drinkable as a rough white wine but is much improved if cask matured for two months.

Red Wine

(Vin Ordinaire)

Ingredients:

1 lb. fresh elderberries (or $\frac{1}{4}$ lb. dried)
1 lb. raisins (or $\frac{1}{4}$ pint red grape concentrate)
1$\frac{1}{2}$ lbs. sugar
1 teaspoon Pektolase or equivalent
Burgundy yeast and nutrient
2 lemons (or $\frac{1}{4}$ oz. citric acid)
Water to 1 gallon

Method:

The ingredients are crushed and placed in a bucket and *boiling* water is poured over them. The water level is brought up to one gallon and when cool the yeast starter and Pektolase are added. The "pulp" is strained off after four days and thereafter fermentation continues in a gallon jar. Rack when all sugar has been used up (generally within a month) and allow to clear. This wine will also improve rapidly if matured in cask for a few months, but in any case can be drunk at six to nine months as a rough table wine similar to the carafe wines of France.

Woodruff

A good old-fashioned favourite. The woodruff is found in woods and shady places especially amongst the leaf mould of beech woods. It flowers in May and June.

Ingredients:

1 gallon woodruff flowers and leaves (no stalks)	2 lemons (or $\frac{1}{4}$ oz. citric acid)
	1 lb. barley (crushed)
3$\frac{1}{2}$ lbs. sugar	1 gallon water
$\frac{1}{2}$ pint cold tea	Activated yeast and nutrient

Method:

Soak and crush the barley and place in fermentation jar with grated lemon rinds (no white pith) and the florets and bruised leaves of the woodruff together with the sugar. Pour in the boiling water, stir to dissolve the sugar and leave to cool. Add the cold tea, lemon juice or citric acid, activated yeast and nutrient. Ferment and rack in the usual way.

Variations may be made by adding chopped raisins (scalded), grape concentrate, Semplex synthetic "must" with adjustment to sugar used.fifi

"And another thing—stop throwing your lees in the flower garden"

Other "AW" Books

C. J. J. Berry

"FIRST STEPS IN WINEMAKING"
—easily the most popular introduction to this fascinating craft. Concise, easily understood, and containing all the complete beginner needs to know. Over 130 reliable recipes, how to use the hydrometer, brewing your own beer, faults in wine, etc., etc.
(6/-) postage 8d.

C. J. J. Berry

"130 NEW WINEMAKING RECIPES"
—the companion book to this one, giving an unrivalled collection of recipes for modern materials (dried fruits, concentrates, etc.). Fifty sparkling cartoons by Rex Royle. (6/-) postage 8d.

C. J. J. Berry

"WINEMAKING WITH CANNED AND DRIED FRUIT"
—the latest and simplest winemaking method of all. All you need is a can-opener! How to make wine from tinned fruits and juices, concentrates, jams, jellies and dried fruit easily obtainable from your grocer or supermarket. Cut out all the drudgery and make wine the easy way. (6/-) postage 8d.

B. Acton and P. Duncan

"MAKING WINES LIKE THOSE YOU BUY"
—how, with your own materials and equipment, to make wines every bit as good as those you have enjoyed on the Continent: Red and White Table Wine, Sauternes, Hock, Moselle, Chianti, Port, Sherry, Madeira, etc., etc. Full range of home-made liqueurs as well. A fascinating book taking you into the finer points of winemaking. Fully illustrated. (6/-) postage 8d.

B. Acton and P. Duncan

"PROGRESSIVE WINEMAKING"
—This magnificent, fact-packed volume by these two popular authors has over 450 pages and is the most comprehensive book on winemaking yet published in this country. Every serious winemaker who aspires to an advanced knowledge of the craft will want it on his shelf. Fully illustrated, strongly bound.
Paperback (15/–) postage 1/6   Hard cover (25/–) postage 1/6

B. Acton and P. Duncan

"MAKING MEAD"
—these two popular authors tell you how to make the oldest alcoholic drink of all, to say nothing of Hippocras, Metheglin, Cyser, Pyments, Melomels and Honey Beers, A book with a lively, fresh approach to an unjustly neglected aspect of winemaking. Illustrated. (5/-) postage 8d.

"JUDGING HOME-MADE WINES AND BEERS"

—the handbook of the National Guild of Judges; constitution, notes for judges, judges' stewards, and show organisers. *How to Judge*, specimen show schedules, etc., etc. Invaluable for those organising competitions.   3/6

(postage 4d.)

C. J. J. Berry and B. C. A. Turner

"THE WINEMAKER'S COMPANION"

—the winemaker's Bible. Comprehensive, attractively produced, and well bound. The best book on the subject for those who want both technical knowledge and readability.   (25/-)

postage 1/6

C. J. J. Berry

"HINTS ON HOME BREWING"

—a "rapid course" on home brewing, but containing all the would-be brewer needs to know. Illustrated.   (2/6) postage 4d.

C. J. J. Berry

"HOME BREWED BEERS AND STOUTS"

—the first and best full-length book on the subject. How to brew your own delicious lager, pale ale, bitter, mild, brown, stout or extra stout. Fully illustrated.   (6/-) postage 8d.

Ken Shales

"BREWING BETTER BEERS"

—a top-notch book by that master brewer from Basildon (alias "the Brewmaster General of Boozeldon"), Ken Shales. A racy, knowledgeable book which tells you how to formulate your own lager, beer and stout recipes, but which also gives Ken's personal recipes for all these brews, for anything from a light lager to an "extra stout" of the sort that's good for you! All these recipes have been tested by his panel of fellow brewers at Basildon and altered or improved until they are 100% satisfactory.   Only 6/-

(postage 8d.)

Gillian Pearkes

"GROWING GRAPES IN BRITAIN"

—a handbook for amateur winemakers. A full-length book for anyone interested in growing "vines for wines", whether just a few on the wall of a house or in a garden, or a full-scale vineyard. Wine grapes *can* be grown and ripened outdoors in Britain, as the author proves by reference to history and to modern viticultural experiments. This is a really detailed viticultural handbook telling you what varieties to plant for success, and full instructions for training, pruning, manuring and cropping vines, both outdoors and in a glasshouse, for propagating vines, for making wine from your home-grown grapes, and for work the whole year round in vineyard, vinery and winey. A fascinating book which will have *you* looking round for a suitable spot to grow a few vines in *your* garden!   (7/6) postage 1/-

T. Edwin Belt

"PRESERVING WINEMAKING INGREDIENTS"

—how to "put down" your surplus ingredients for future use by drying, bottling, deep-free;ing or chemical methods. How to make syrups, jams and jellies. 6/–

(postage 8d.)

J. R. Mitchell

"SCIENTIFIC WINEMAKING—MADE EASY"

—This is without doubt the most advanced and informative book so far available to the winemaker and is one which every serious devotee of the craft will want to own. Despite the wealth of scientific and background knowledge it contains, it has a practical down-to-earth approach. The aim of the book is to do what virtually no other book does, to give *precise* instructions and methods for producing particular types of wines to close specifications, **well-balanced** wines of assured quality. The author, himself a quality control manager with a large group of companies with wine interests in this country, sets out the tests and procedures that *you* can adopt to ensure quality in your wines, and does so in a simple and explicit manner. This will inevitably become a standard book of reference in the winemaking world; **there is no other book like it.** (12/-) postage 1/-

Tilly Timbrell and Bryan Acton

"THE WINEMAKER'S COOKBOOK"

—The only book of its kind on the market. How to cook a whole range of soups, hors d'oeuvres, fish, poultry and meat dishes, desserts, cakes and gateaux using your own country wines. A feast of a book! (7/-) postage 8d.

Drs. F. Beech and A. Pollard

WINEMAKING and BREWING

—An authoritative book by these two experts from the Long Ashton Research Station. It covers the whole subject thoroughly in most practical fashion. (7/-) postage 8d.

INDEX

INDEX

INDEX

INDEX